CRISP BLUE EDGES:

Indigenous Creative Non-Fiction

CRISP BLUE EDGES:

Indigenous Creative Non-Fiction

Edited by Rasunah Marsden

Theytus Books Ltd.
Penticton, BC

Canadian Cataloguing in Publication Data
Main entry under title:
Crisp blue edges

ISBN 0-919441-92-0
1. Native peoples–Canada–Literary collections.* 2. Canadian literature (English)–Indian authors.* 3. Canadian literature (English)–20th century.* I. Marsden, Rasunah, 1949-
PS8235.I6C75 2000   C810.8'0897   C00-911142-5
PR9194.5.I5C75 2000

ACKNOWLEDGEMENTS
Editorial Committee: Rasunah Marsden, Jeannette Armstrong, Drew Hayden Taylor
Book Design & Layout: Florene Belmore
Cover Design: August Armstrong, Florene Belmore, Rasunah Marsden
Typesetting: Karen Olsen, Chick Gabriel
Proof Reading: Audrey Huntley, Chick Gabriel
Cover Photo: August Armstrong
Special Thanks: Turning Earth Productions, August Armstrong, Tracey Bonneau-Jack
Title "Crisp Blue Edges" taken from Jeannette Armstrong, Whispering in Shadows, (Penticton, Theytus Books, 2000) p. 287

Theytus Books Ltd.
Lot 45, Green Mountain Rd.
RR #2, Site 50, Comp. 8
Penticton, BC
V2A 6J7

The publisher acknowledges the support of The Canada Council for the Arts, The Department of Canadian Heritage and The British Columbia Arts Council.

TABLE OF CONTENTS

FOREWARD

by Jeannette Armstrong

The idea of having an Indigenous Creative Non-Fiction Forum came in a conversation with Rasunah Marsden over how we should define an Aboriginal approach to the Non-Fiction course we were offering at The En'owkin International School of Writing. In that discussion to develop course materials and to identify Aboriginal writings which fell into that genre, we began an interesting academic critical dialogue which we both felt needed to be enriched by those who were writing from that genre.

We discussed examples of writing which somehow could not be categorized as fiction, poetry, drama or standard non-fiction. We had already begun to recognize that many works by Aboriginal writers were grounded in orality, and meant to be spoken or performed. As well, we found academic non-fiction works constructed as narrative story and wonderful examples of journalism presented in a storytelling style. Our discussion carried us into the terrain of how we might read and approach such works with the motivation of identifying commonalities.

Rasunah was clear that no text was available which covered the various approaches we found in the examples which proliferated in various journals and publications. It became clear that creating a collection would be an important resource for reference by writers as well as instructors and would greatly contribute to our work in pointing out that Aboriginal Literatures require their own pedagogical approach.

As academics and writers engaged in facilitating the appreciation of Aboriginal Literatures in En'owkin's creative writing program, we shared an interest in contributing to an on-going dialogue among our colleagues and peers towards a developing pedagogy focused on Aboriginal Literatures. It occurred to us that we required a process which would deconstruct the standard and assist in the collective articulation of some guiding principles.

The idea of having an actual dialogue with writers of the genre grew out of our own dialogue in which we found ourselves building on each other's thinking to identify and develop clarity around our own ideas. Rasunah asked why we couldn't find some money to bring a peer group of Aboriginal writers together to have a dialogue on what creative non-fiction from their perspectives might be.

This book became a project headed by Rasunah. The Canada Council for the Arts funded the organization of The Forum which was held at The Trade and Convention Centre in Penticton on March 21, 1998. The dialogue was facilitated by Rasunah as a roundtable dialogue in the First Nations Circle style, which gives each participant in the circle an opportunity to speak. The circle dialogue format also creates a consensus building which is collaborative in the outcome. The dialogue was exciting in that the peers were high profile Aboriginal writers who were articulate and conversant with a critical approach to Aboriginal Literatures. The invited peers were Lee Maracle, Kateri Akiwenzie-Damm, Sandra Laronde, Jeannette Armstrong, Drew Hayden Taylor, Maria Campbell, Greg Young-Ing and Rasunah Marsden.

During the morning there was general discussion on the topic of Indigenous creative non-fiction; while in the afternoon, invited participants read their work. Observers were invited to contribute in an open session. The session was video-taped by Turning Earth Productions so that at some future point a video might be made. Karen Olsen, a senior En'owkin student, transcribed the dialogue. We decided that preserving the dynamics of the dialogue as a collaborative oral process was important to the project. We also decided that it would be important to include others who could not be physically present at the dialogue by sending out a Call for Submissions for the inclusion in this collection.

I found it to be one of the most intensive and exhilarating projects in which I have participated. The variety of approaches identified in the collaborative process provided a clarity which needed to be shared. It offered innovative ways of academically looking at reality and perception. It revealed to us the importance of oral storytelling and the positioning of narrator drawing on mythological character. Oral rhetoric and commentary, usually dismissed from literary genre, became central to discussion on style and strengthened our resolve to maintain our pedagogical position of their literary importance. We found comfort in developing a clearer view of those works which blur the lines between poetry and prose and use internal devices usually reserved for performance. The value of writing reality as voice revealed to us how Aboriginal voices which work in this genre provide ways of perceiving story arising out of community concerned with connection in real space. Most of all, the integrity of the collective and collaborative process seeking inclusivity, deconstructing the rigidity of categorizations, was worth the work of bringing the forum together and creating this collection.

Thanks to all the organizers, participating and contributing authors and to The Canada Council for supporting both the organization of the project and the publication of this book.

Light Will Break Over the Crisp Blue Edges of the Mountains: Indigenous Creative Non-Fiction in the WYSIWYG Era

by Rasunah Marsden

I come to creative non-fiction from several different angles, but mainly through straddling two activities: that of the writer of poetry and that of a teacher. As a creative writing teacher I focus in a critical dialogue about creative non-fiction by asking what relationships lie between the form and content and whether or not the form of non-fiction is an extension of its content, bearing in mind that an imbalance between form and content muddies the overall intent and impact of writing. *For instance,* there is writing that is high in technique and style, but leaves no impact, because nothing memorable has been written. And there is writing that one struggles through to find the gem or richness of a thought or experience, which defies all impressions of what comprises a good piece of writing. But then as a writer I will heave out all that nonsense because I have the understanding that the best writing defies analysis, that is, it will be writing whose structure may not easily be unraveled, and whose creative source may only be savoured.

EXCERPT #1.

We are comfortable on the rich grass stolen from arid beauty, and watch the sun beat on an ensemble of singers and dancers from a horse people from the north who aren't used to the heat.

They illustrate different dances to the crowd, who were fooled into thinking there's nothing left, but songs are a cue as to what walks among the unseen. Ancestors stand with jackrabbit and saquaro—all of us beneath the flight of dipping hawks.

The drum makes a wedge into consciousness before the flute player begins melodic flight on notes based on a scale that has nothing to do with the construction of a piano in Europe.

This scale involves the relationship of the traveller's horse to the morning star and what the arc makes as it lovingly re-creates red dawn.

Somewhere far from here it is raining as steady as the patter the grass makes and it has been raining hard for years.

The hawk makes an elegant scribble in the wing of mist and within this story is the flute player who acquires the secret of flying.

I hear the opening of the Bear Dance I saw performed at the Holiday Inn in Reno. Suddenly bears converged in that conference room as slot machines rang up pitiful gains and losses. We joined the bear world as they danced for us, the same as we join the dancers spiraling from this lawn.

We have always been together.

* * * *

My son called me once at three in the morning. I could not sleep after the call, worrying for him and wondered once again about the wisdom of bringing children into the world who will suffer. A child's suffering always finds the most tender place in the heart, and a woman's children, though grown humans, will always be children.

Yet there's revelation in suffering, like the history in the song I heard the day after the call from a Plains group who performed on the lawn of the university.

Within that song was the beauty of horses. My son's name means lover of horses.[1]

The word 'non-fiction' is problematic because it connotes a semblance to fact, observation, and various recognizable forms of structure, journalism, academe, communications, popular and autobiographical writing *& the list goes on*. Added to that, the term 'creative' non-fiction is both a relief and an exasperation. We know that non-fiction is prose. *So far, so good.* We know that poetic prose is exactly what it says it is—prose whose style is poetic. But how closely aligned to poetic prose is non-fiction? Probably not much aligned. To creative non-fiction? It could be that there are a great many similarities between poetic prose and creative non-fiction. But what kind, and where do the similarities end?

In order to demonstrate what I mean, lets look at three pieces of writing. The previous excerpt was from Joy Harjo's book The Woman Who Fell From The Sky, the second is from Linda Hogan's book Dwellings and the third is from Jeannette Armstrong's Whispering in Shadows. Before I examine these excerpts, however, I will also discuss some relevant issues. *(Readers are hereafter cautioned and encouraged to draw their own conclusions by consulting the author's whole works.)*

Before I "go there" (as some of my students might put it), it should be stated that Indigenous non-fiction has come a long way. Earlier Indigenous writing was more autobiographical, and of a journal or diary style, with less tendency to creative flight. There was the usual changing of names of characters who were in reality person's known to the writer, but little else would conceal the fact that a non-fiction spouse or relative described in early non-fiction and a spouse or relative in real life were one and the same. Today in contemporary creative non-fiction such a convention may be ignored for any number of reasons, including the protection of a person or group's identity. Put another way, it often occurs that characters/people are secondary to what is dealt with in a lot of creative non-fiction. Today there is a preference for themes which are topical and brief, and which deal with perception. In this way, creative non-fiction has become less object and data oriented, less strictly or chronologically or matter-of-factly organized and more experimental. You could say that the state of contemporary, creative non-fiction is, in effect, transitional and experimental. Maybe even more process than object-oriented in flow and treatment. *(Of course, these are only my observations.)*

As for my invented phrase 'object-oriented non-fiction' (from the immediate post-war era), this type of older non-fiction writing was 'stylistic' in format, and much of the range of stylized non-fiction techniques used by writers began to go out of fashion along with devices such as: the limits and advantages of first or third person points of view; and the fact that information needed to be presented in 'digestible' sophisticated ways, so long as you had a beginning, middle and end, etc. Then the pendulum swung the other way in mainstream especially North American circles, until you got to the 'new journalism' stage, for which the parallel in developments in non-fiction would be equally 'bad' non-fiction writing which abandoned ALL stylistic devices in favor of the "Me" generation's bubble gum approach—anything goes and let's dispense with objectivity and absolute accuracy. Skewing and skewering is IN!

So where Indigenous writers seem to be at the moment is in the process of making our own creative sense out of unfashionable legacies in writing styles which we inherited from public and tertiary school systems and mainstream media. To refer back to the descriptors that creative non-fiction today is "transitional and experimental," I don't know if nowadays non-fiction is creative because it is 'experimental' or experimental because it is more creative, *but hopefully you get my historical drift. It remains to be said that* perceptive and process-oriented non fiction is also indicative of what writers find acceptable as creative non-fiction today.

Excerpt #2.

John Hay, in The Immortal Wilderness, has written: "There are occasions when you can hear the mysterious language of the Earth, in water, or coming through the trees, emanating from the mosses, seeping through the undercurrents of the soil, but you have to be willing to wait and receive." Sometimes I hear it talking. The light of the sunflower was one language, but there are others more audible. Once, in the redwood forest, I heard a beat, something like a drum or heart coming from the ground and trees and wind. That underground current stirred a kind of knowing inside me, a kinship and longing, a dream barely remembered that disappeared back to the body. Another time, there was the booming voice of an ocean storm thundering from far out at sea, telling about what lived in the distance, about the rough water that would arrive, wave after wave revealing the disturbance at center.

Tonight I walk. I am watching the sky. I think of the people who came before me and how they knew the placement of stars in the sky, watched the moving sun long and hard enough to witness how a certain angle of light touched a stone only once a year. Without written records, they knew the gods of every night, the small, fine details of the world around them and of immensity above them.

Walking, I can almost hear the redwoods beating. And the oceans are above me here, rolling clouds, heavy and dark, considering snow. On the dry, red road, I pass the place of the sunflower, that dark and secret location where creation took place. I wonder if it will return this summer, if it will multiply and move up to the other stand of flowers in a territorial struggle.

It's winter and there is smoke from the fires. The square, lighted windows of houses are fogging over. It is a world of elemental attention, of all things working together, listening to what speaks in the blood. Whichever road I follow, I walk in the land of many gods, and they love and eat one another. Walking, I am listening to a deeper way. Suddenly all my ancestors are behind me. Be still, they say. Watch and listen. You are the result of the love of thousands."[2]

Wait, I'm not finished. The genre of creative non-fiction has also expanded and become more versatile. There is a whole range of non-fiction which previously did not exist. This includes a proliferation of things like commentaries or anecdotally-based pieces which are socio-political yet playful, opinionated or provocative, and usually of a short length of only a few pages. It includes things like reflective pieces which are little more than anecdotal musings on the tidbits of the day, certainly not inspiringly philosophical in nature. It also includes, in Indigenous circles, such things as 'identity' pieces primarily devoted to either the individual's or group's search, preoccupation and analysis of the contemporary Indigenous perspective, contrasted with the dubious legacy of colonialism. We of the WYSIWYG (What You See Is What You Get) era are nevertheless resolved that we are free to create any form of creative non-fiction that we like...

And that is exactly what is happening.

Excerpt #3.

This night will be long, filled with morose shadows gathering around.

Finally, weak and tired after singing all the songs she knows, she sinks down to rest for a few moments before sitting up to sing again. Her eyes are heavy and she can't keep them open. She dreams.

The bear is moving. It stands up on its fours. It turns to face her. Snuffling at her. Then it slowly lifts its great paws and stands on its hind legs. Slowly it begins to sway, dancing. At first it is dark, like the night, then it begins to turn a silvery color like the stars. The stars' spines are shooting down into the bear and the bear is glowing like starlight. Its eyes are stars. The bear dances, making motions with its hands, to come. She stands too and feels as light as air. She can hear the man from Mexico talking. The bear is now the Aztec man from Mexico, and he is talking to her. "We came from the stars," he said. "The gateway is just ahead. Already many people come from all directions to it. See this candle in the middle. It shines a light touching everyone who comes to its fire. Shining Woman of Copper, your light is the silvery tears even now catching the starlight. Your love of life. All your friends and your children gather close to its light. When the wind takes the candle's light, its fire is only moved to another. The Great Bear walks across the sky at night. In dreams and shadows. Without the night, no stars would sing their songs. You can dance in the star's light, too." Suddenly she sees the world from high up in the sky. The sky is dark with clouds and she feels like she is a cloud, too, but she can see the world below. It is dark and shadowy but she can see tiny pinpoints of light scattered across the land. At first she thinks they are cities, but she moves close and sees they are circles from all over the earth. Laughing and talking as coyotes shrill their songs around them. "Oh Coyote," she says, "you can't reach the stars. Don't you know, by now, that they'll cut the strings?' Coyote sits down and laughs looking up at her.

He points his nose up toward her and howls. "Shining Woman of Copper. You know it's in the story. Every story. It's just the same old monsters again. I'll take care of them bastards, though. Piss on them. It's gotta be. Just keep on shining 'till the sun sets. You're free to ride the clouds. I am the greatest chief down around here and I will give you that."

Penny wakes up with a start. A coyote is shrilling a song close by. She shivers thinking of her dream and laughs out loud. It is cold and dark but she feels rested and deep inside there is a feeling of bubbling upward.

The night will reach its darkest soon and it will be long. But it is always darkest just before the dawn's first light. And then the bright shafts of light will break over the crisp blue edges of the mountains towering to the east, and the world will be new.[3]

I realize there are a few strange things going on around here, including the way this article is structured. Never mind. It will all come clear in the end, so keep going. To the discerning literary analyst, Excerpt #1 has to be poetic prose. It might be something out of a novel because third person starts it off, but it immediately switches to the first person, with a decidedly journalistic, contemplative and explanatory tone. So we are not going to rely on pronouns to make any further decisions about whether the piece is autobiographical, from a novel, or a collection of poetry. As for setting and time frame, these are slippery items, as the writer persona seems to be suspended between the past and present.

Looks promising. The second excerpt uses a quote, perhaps we can use this as a clue. Someone is doing some walking in a dubious time frame. The tone is also contemplative and sense impressions outline connections between walking and what associations are made by "I." There is a lot of attention being paid in this excerpt to sounds—the talking of sunflowers, a beat from the ground, an ocean storm, and redwoods—as though these elements "speak" through the walker, "telling" of "what lives in the distance" of "knowing the gods of every night" and "the place of the sunflower, that dark and secret location where creation took place." In Excerpt #1, the dancers from the bear world, those sitting, the traveller's horse, those in the sky and the ancestors, are as unified and connected as are those which inform the landscape, in which the walker and what is "walked" is one with "a deeper way"—a way in which there is no sense of separation, neither from the visible or the invisible world in which all of the walker's ancestors are present. As the "result of the love of thousands" the walker embodies all that unfolds upon her path, and all that is on her path unfolds her. But all this begins to sound mysterious, even spiritual. We are no longer sure that Excerpt #2 can be classified as non-fiction. 'Imaginative' or creative non-fiction, maybe. *No real point in stretching notions of what we think creative non-fiction is, is there? (Tsk, Tsk! The reality business. Especially nowadays.)*

Aha... at last in Excerpt #3 we have to be home-free. This HAS to be creative non-fiction. Why? Partially because the writer accounts in detail of a personal experience, someone's personal experience. Granted, the person who is having this experience in the excerpt could be fictional but somehow we doubt it. She might as well have been a number of people I can think of who have spent a few days in the woods. Alone. And why would anyone bother to fictionalize such a thing in the first place? Admittedly, the person is dreaming, and the dream, if complete with howling coyotes as you would expect any dream from the Okanagan would be, is dutifully detailed by the author. Storyland, shadows—the dream is full of everything imaginable, no stone left unturned, so-to-speak. *(The dream itself seems to deserve a coyote in it.)* After the dreamer wakes, the writing turns again to further reflection in the 2nd italicized section of the excerpt. As anyone knows, today non-fiction heaves with 'personalized,' subjective reflections. which, especially in Excerpt #3, can hardly be written by any but of one whose accounts are grounded in, and are an exposition of, experience...

Well... Writers know that biographers are obliged to fictionalize some of the experience of their subjects. We can safely assume that autobiographers do a little of the same beating around the bush. The names are changed. Everything has changed. *(Except the meaning or the truth, perhaps, or simply our perception of it?)* We know that non-fiction writers are supposed to use accurate details of setting, person, event, but they don't. We know that all writers are guilty of fictionalizing as much as possible, or at least wherever possible... and in truth, writers have bent everything out of shape. A scientist may say, "We know the properties of a glass vessel," but I have to add, "But my God, what a <u>beautiful</u> glass vessel." *(Writers have bent glass vessels out of shape also.)* We used to be able to label one form of vessel as a novel, another a short story, and so on and so forth. But there is still some light at the end of the tunnel. You could argue that there is less uniformity and that the shape of things to come will be even less comprehensible. But it also could just as easily be understood that the style, shape and classification of writing has dramatically opened up, and that we writers no longer take as much notice of things like conventional, suffocating styles which formerly have been everyone else's bread and butter.

It is obvious that the shape, truth and style of good writing are no longer issues for classification, although I realize some publishers may hang onto such classifications as though they were pieces of gold. It should be obvious that, just as one swallow does not make a summer, style and format do not creative non-fiction make. It should be obvious that emergent creative non-fiction defies former methods and definitions of writing practice in that same field. And, that any number of works of Indigenous creative non-fiction are much richer in overlap of stylistic concerns and devices than they ever were, for all of the heavy borrowing done and treaties made with poetry, poetic prose, fiction, and not least of all, drama, for singularly innovative and creative purposes. *It reminds me of the phrase, "the 1001 Nights" but let's speak of the "veils of perception" instead like this: "Can you be sure, Columbus, that what you saw was a novel, a bunch of short stories, a creative non-fiction collection, or what?"*

Most obvious, the state of literary criticism, the fundamentals of which have been imposed upon the wary and unsuspecting since the first public high school doors were opened, has fallen into disrepute. There are reasons for this. *And I know I can hear the writing students replying insistently to the genie, "But who cares?"* But the point remains that, partially due to a lack of contemporary critical perspectives, creative non-fiction writing has run off down the road with the vegetable cart, leaving most would-be critics behind. Excerpt #3's classification is as yet undecided, Excerpt #2's classification was nowhere to be found on the book jacket (rather, it is "lyrically written musings on the nature of nature" or "wisdom literature") and Excerpt #1 is described as "a volume of poetry." *I kid you not.* If it is no longer possible to determine what a piece of writing IS *(and if the author refuses to classify, how will you?)* from noting point of view, use of pronouns, real experiences, styles of prose, formats and structure or time frames and settings are contained in the document, upon what basis are we going to decide what 'creative non-fiction' IS?

For the skeptical, only one of the above-mentioned excerpts is creative non-fiction.

(But I know you already know which one it is.)

* * * *

Footnotes

(1) "Sonata For The Invisible" Joy Harjo, <u>The Woman Who Fell From The Sky</u>,(New York: W.W. Norton & Co., 1994)p.49-50

(2) "Walking" Linda Hogan, <u>Dwellings</u>, (New York: A Touchstone Book, Simon & Shuster, 1996) p.158

(3) Jeannette Armstrong, <u>Whispering in Shadows</u>,(Penticton: Theytus Books 2000) p. 286-287

Acknowledgement: Title "Light Will Break Over the Crisp Blue Edges of the Mountains" taken from Jeannette Armstrong, <u>Whispering in Shadows</u>,(Penticton: Theytus Books 2000) p. 287

PART I

Speaking in the Round

Transcript of the Indigenous Creative Non-Fiction Forum

Lee Maracle: I have been named a creative non-fiction writer. I believe that I play with memory. I believe that memory serves, that memory has direction and that from that original direction people keep adding new knowledge to the original direction. My original direction is a Salish direction. I come from a speaking culture; so much of my work is still from the oral. I struggle to keep it that way because the tendency is to get swallowed by the definitions. I struggle to stay in the context which I was in originally.

Kateri Akiwenzie-Damm: I'm from the Chippewas in Ontario on the banks of the beautiful Saugeen Peninsula. In terms of my attraction to this genre, I think for me it began when I was at the University of Ottawa. I was studying literature there and I took a course, which I had to take, on the Romantics, and I absolutely despised it. I hated the discussions. The University of Ottawa is not a university where I saw a lot of cultural or ethnic diversity. For me it was mainly a bunch of white students sitting around talking about concepts of the universal mind, universal this and universal that, which totally excluded everything I was thinking about. So I was sitting there thinking, this is not universal at all. I had a lot of trouble speaking in that class because my points were not accepted by the students and the Prof. So I just got more and more frustrated, to the point where, when it came to the time that I had to hand in my final essay, I absolutely refused to do an academic essay. I was so angry and I wanted to express the idea that I was outside of the dialogue that had gone on in the classroom and to do that I broke all the rules for an academic essay. I used autobiography. I used the first person. I included poetry. I said whatever I wanted to say in absolute frustration with the whole process. I think that's when I started to really make a commitment to write non-fiction, and even academic essays, in a way that didn't force me to wear a mask that I didn't want to wear, or force me to think in a way that was foreign to me. Since then I've been attempting to do that. For me it means putting heart even into academics, putting passion into academic essays and not letting go of the kinds of things that I want to say, in the ways that I want to express them. That's more or less how I got involved in this and what I've been attempting to do with my work. I hadn't actually thought of it with that term 'creative non-fiction' until this forum. I never really used that term.

Sandra Laronde: I'm from the Teme-Augama Anishnaabe in Temagami, Northern Ontario. When I walked into a bookstore on Queen Street, I said, "Do you have a copy of <u>Lame Deer, Seeker of Visions</u>?" He said, "Oh, I'm sorry we don't have a mythology section here." And that was interesting because as soon as they hear the word 'visions' and certain other words, they think of fiction, mythology and new age. That other world isn't part of their thinking. This is just a simple act of going to buy a book. I think that creative non-fiction has something to do with that. Something to do with bringing those worlds together, what is called the material world, the natural world and the so-called supernatural world. I think it has something to do with a bridging of different realms. I'm working on a piece right now called *"N'Daki Menan."* It means "our homeland" in Anishnaabe. It's about a journey, which is partly creative non-fiction. It's a journey motif of a woman at the centre of the world. Here one meets and encounters the Root Woman. Below the ancient pine trees of Temagami, in the roots that spiral down into the earth, lives this Root Woman. She only surfaces when destruction is nearby. She is like a tree living in different realms all at once: in the underworld below the earth, the sky world and earth world. Creative non-fiction involves the weaving of memory and even forgetting. We work to retrieve and uncover silences, to bring it to the surface as The Root Woman brings knowledge to the surface. I come from a theatre background where I was trained to know that memory sits right in the body and you can access the memory of the body to reveal its stories. They may even be stories beyond your lifetime and I think writing is about that retrieval.

Jeannette Armstrong: I'm not really sure anyone knows what creative non-fiction is. I think that's one of the reasons we wanted to have this dialogue, because we get a lot of different versions of it. I think it's really exciting because it is a genre that seems to be something that a lot of Native people use. I'm a writer and I also come from an oral and traditional storytelling tradition. For me, whenever we are talking about legends, we are talking about non-fiction because our stories come from our people. Now the non-natives might call it mythology or legend but it's a history and a tracking of our people in terms of their intellectual discoveries, historical discoveries, science discoveries—all of that. So I'm interested in looking at how we might think about it, analyze it and so on. In all the time that I've been working at the (En'owkin) Centre and working with Lee and other writers back in the sixties and seventies, I remember picking up and reading any newspaper, anything that was written by Native people and a lot of it was creative non-fiction—rather than journalism or rather than something classified as non-fiction. I also remember (my husband) Marlowe talking to me one time and telling me, "I couldn't do English literature very well because my instructor told me that I just write how I talk." I thought, "That's it. That's it! That's what we do." You find a lot of Native people who are speaking from the narrative in their writing and so it becomes creative non-fiction in that they're telling a story and they're telling it from a first person narrative point of view. You can see and hear the person who is telling the story. Their presence is there. I think that's an important aspect of some of the things we want to talk about today. It personalizes and we might need to think about how pedagogy is handling this.

I'm currently working on my second novel. It will be published this year. Like Lee Maracle's novel and Maria Campbell's novel, a lot of <u>Slash</u> (my first novel) is not only autobiographical but is also non-fiction. I would say eighty-five percent of it is non-fiction and fifteen percent of it is fiction. The part that's fictionalized is the main character who carries the story but the rest of it is all non-fiction. All of it is historically true, documented, things that we know about in our communities and so on. So, is it a fiction piece? No, it isn't. That has been some of the critical dialogue around <u>Slash</u>. It's got all of those literary critics scratching their heads and saying, "What is this? What is Lee's novel?"

Drew Hayden Taylor: I'm from Curve Lake First Nation in Central Ontario. My connection to creative non-fiction is that I originally started out as a journalist working with CBC and writing for several newspapers and radio shows. I always had a problem with straight journalism, straight non-fiction, because I always felt I could write better quotes than the ones people would give me and editors tend to frown on that. I hated relying on other people to tell me a good story. So as a result I drifted away from writing straight non-fiction because it didn't really appeal to me. I went through several different career choices in my life, and ended up as a playwright and writing for television. But there was always something in it about writing about the world around me—as I perceive it rather than fictionalizing it. So I ended up writing a series of articles for various newspapers that used the journalism training that I had but giving it a slightly ironic, unusual twist, sort of first person singular type of approach. What I do has been very successful. The first anthology of my articles was published into a book called Funny You Don't Look Like One: Observations of a Blue-Eyed Ojibway.

What I do, when I write, when I create creative non-fiction, is reinterpret reality. As a fiction and a non-fiction writer, I always found reality is far more interesting than anything I could ever write. So when I sit down and write these things I look at the world around me, at things that are happening, and I think, "okay, lets give it a different spin and look at it in a different, unusual, new perspective." And that basically is what comes out of it for me and why I enjoy writing. It's something fun.

Maria Campbell: I'm Métis, Cree from Saskatchewan. I also have never thought about creative non-fiction. I've never thought of myself as that kind of a writer. In fact, I'm just starting now to get used to thinking about myself as a writer. I'm a storyteller and I'm very comfortable with that term because it has allowed me to be moved in all kinds of directions. When I think of creative non-fiction I think of somebody writing books and only a particular kind of book. I like to work with theatre. I like to work with plays and I like working in film. All over, whatever is available for whatever I have to talk about. Because sometimes the story I want to tell doesn't work in a book. Or it doesn't work in a magazine or a play but it will work in a video. I like the freedom of working around mediums because when I think of writing being classed as fiction and non-fiction I sort of feel trapped. If I were thinking about it, I don't think I could write creative non-fiction. As soon as I think of a classification I get stuck and I get blocked and I can't work. I've always had problems with things like titles. I think of things that blocked me as a child, things that had power and authority over my life. Although I think I'm a big girl and I've sort of ditched all that stuff it still pops up in terms like that.

I think about a voice, somebody coming into me, someone who wants to tell me a story, whether it's a tree or a situation that's happening between you and somebody else. Or I'm walking somewhere on my own land. Or even like Sandra (Laronde) says your body has memory and stories. I think of that as being. So when I think that way I'm very comfortable and it's not scary. I just think somebody wants to tell a story and here I am, just the interpreter or translator. But this last year has been interesting because I've decided to become a graduate student. I did that for a couple of reasons. The main one being I found that when I was teaching creative writing and drama and Oral Tradition, there was a space between my students and me. I couldn't understand some of the places that they were talking about because most of them didn't speak a (Native) language. They'd been raised in the city, and they had been in university for a long time, by the time they ended up in my class. I didn't understand a lot of their language and I felt that I had a lot to give them. Not so much that I had a lot, but I had been given a lot, and I could pass it on to other students. So I decided to go back to school.

I was very fortunate in that I was accepted as a graduate student, something I had asked for. They recognized all the teaching that I'd had from people in my own community. I'm also known as a traditional storyteller, an Oral Tradition storyteller. Those were the buzzwords at that time. They recognized that and that's how I was able to get into a Master's program, so what I'm finding is that I'm looking at stories in a whole new way. When I'm sitting down with my own teachers I'm asking them different kinds of questions than I was asking before which is really good for me and very good for them. Because I wouldn't have thought about that before. So I think it's going to make me a better teacher than I used to be. I'm doing lots of writing. I should be doing academic writing but I found that I couldn't write anything academic for a couple of years. I finished my play.

So I have the first draft of a play done. It's called "Negotiations." It happens in a room at a negotiation table. The government on this side and the people on that side. I don't quite know what's going to happen with that. I need to workshop it. And I have a collection of poetry and short stories that are my own creative writing that is ready to be published but I need to get an editor to work on the poetry with me. I've got another batch of translations too, so I'm not running out of stuff. And the good thing is that my creative stuff is much stronger than it was before. It's really just in need of a lot of translation. So it will be interesting to see what's going to happen with the writing. What I've found from my studies this year is that I really like Post-Modernism. I hadn't even thought about that before and I've come to the conclusion that Crees and Métis were Post-Modernists before anyone else. Because it's really the only thing in academia that I've found I could relate to. It's very much the way that all of us think. Oh, some of it is off the wall but so is anything else. So that's an interest. So I'll have this new lingo maybe.

Greg Young-Ing: I'm the Managing Editor for Theytus Books. Like a lot of people here this forum made me think about what creative non-fiction is, and the first thing I thought was that it's something that a lot of non-Aboriginal writers are just recently starting to do. I mean the term—creative non-fiction—is a relatively new term, what ten years ago the academic world would have seen as an oxymoron. But now, as a lot of writers are starting to do it, Aboriginal and non-Aboriginal, it's becoming a recognized term. Maybe it will become a recognized genre someday. So I think back to the first books by Aboriginal authors that came out in the early sixties and seventies and most of them were creative non-fiction—although the term wasn't used back then. For example <u>The Fourth World</u> by George Manuel, Maria Campbell's <u>Halfbreed</u>, Harold Cardinal's <u>Unjust Society</u> and Howard Adam's <u>Prison of Grass</u>. They were talking about political, social and cultural issues, but they were also telling stories of their own lives and how the two blended together. There was even some storytelling in those books. So it was creative non-fiction. That tradition has continued to the present day and Aboriginal authors have always blended genres. I think it comes from the Oral Tradition, partly. Another thing I think it comes from is that, as Aboriginal Peoples, one thing that distinguishes us from others is that we have a sense of multi-levels of reality in our lives. The so-called legends are seen as fiction, folklore tales by other people. But it is creative non-fiction writing because of the multi-levels of reality. I think it's a lot more interesting than the established genre of non-fiction. I'm a little bit of a writer myself but not so much since I started publishing. I also thought back, like Kateri, when I was doing my first Masters paper—and I say that because I'm doing my second one right now—when I was at Carleton University I was doing a thesis. I called it Of the Earth: An Aboriginal Perspective of Aboriginal Rights. There was another Cree student, Peter Coon, who was writing his thesis at the same time and he was a good friend of mine. He was in many of my classes and we started talking about how we wanted to use things Elders and our grandparents told us, things that we heard in political speeches, in our thesis because that's what had meaning to us and that's the knowledge that meant the most to us that we could apply in an academic paper. Of course, we did a lot of reading too. But for both of us, to use Elders' words and other oral sources in our footnotes, we had to argue with our professor and our committee. In the end they allowed us to do that and it ended up in my paper, and in Peter's too, that over half of our footnotes were not from books. So I had a similar experience to Kateri's in that way.

Maria Campbell: It's the same for all of us in universities. Back home there are about six different levels of stories and each one level has a different name and each one has specific training that goes with it. So when you look at fiction, non-fiction, all of those categories, we have all of those in our own languages too. There is fiction and non-fiction in Cree for sure. Those are the two main ones, but there are other types of stories as well. They each have a name and special characteristics that make them different.

Lee Maracle: I just want to say something about naming. If you clear the path of all the names you previously were handed, and if you really look at or research yourself in relationship to all of creation and name yourself in that context, you see that we've been handed a set of names and they all have race-based, colonial-based, conquest-based meanings. And the assumption is that the others out there get to name things. Creative non-fiction arises out of us having published and other world peoples having published work coming from multi-levels of reality. The colonizer people come from a conquest background so that's the direction they always travel in. So they hurry to name it so that we can't name it ourselves. In that way they can accept it. They can't accept something they haven't conquered. So if they name it, define it and apply the rules to it, then they own it and we just fit into it.

I resist the name 'creative non-fiction' because it makes no sense. For me what makes sense is breath, wind, voice and memory. I've been playing with this for my next novel. It's about direction, it's about voice, about the wind, and it's about breath and memory. The very moment that a thought is complete it becomes a memory. Whether the event occurred or not doesn't matter. It becomes a memory and it becomes part of the direction you travel in. You have direction and this direction is an original direction. This body memory that the theatre works with is not something outside of our understanding of the body. It is one of our contributions to the world of the body. You have a body memory. You have an original direction. You travel in that direction no matter what levels of reality you come from. You still respond to that reality in a directive kind of way.

So memory then is what this is about. It can serve the creation of story. It can serve poetry. It can serve our sociology. It can serve an economy. It can serve interpreting reality. It can serve many things, but it's about memory. And it's about the expression of memory and we can choose how to express the memory. We do mix up genres. If this works best I'd pull it in because it's our house, it's our memory. We are making it serve us in ways that we choose. I think it's about memory, not about creative non-fiction. We have to get into the habit of putting our breath into our own things and naming things ourselves because that's where the distortion occurs and the perception of ourselves occurs.

Maria Campbell: It's different if you've have been working with the oral stories because that's not your own. The rules then are actually much stricter than they are if you are working with English. You know, like fiction writers or playwrights have things that they have to work within. I have the hardest time with film because they say you have to have a beginning, middle and ending as a part of the structure. And you know that's where I get caught up doing creative writing, coming from working with Oral Tradition. Because Oral Tradition is so precise and so strict, the Elders are really strict. You can't get creative. There are times when I really want to get creative with something that I'm translating, but I can't touch it. I have to be really true to the way that it is. I have to make sure that I don't take any pieces of it and work it into something I'm working on, on my own. There are those stories and then there are my own. Sometimes I feel almost schizophrenic. I'm coming from a place that's a real strict place, and then I have freedom over here to be able to be creative.

Lee Maracle: There's a thing that happens when we tell our stories. When we hear a story and a person delivers it, it's like a song. A song that delivers this story exactly as the original story was handed to us. Then we are called upon to see ourselves in this story and to own it and make it our own. And from it chart a direction in our lives. Those oral stories are laws. We can't change the law. We have to behave in a certain way, and those stories are meant to be articulated exactly as they are handed to you. But once you have absorbed it, once you've swallowed the information, you can use it to chart your life. It governs your creativity.

Maria Campbell: But the Oral Tradition determines where it's going to go. You don't determine where it goes.

Lee Maracle: Right, it determines where you go. It becomes your direction and it directs all your work. It's your stone that you are standing on. That's the original memory that we have and from that all our beings arise. And what about what we forget? "I can't remember how to fill out a form for the life of me." What we forget is significant too. If somebody tells me how ribonucleic acid happens in the body, I'll remember it because it's about well-being. What we remember, what we forget is directed by original memory which is our law. You don't change the stone, the rock you're standing on. You just move in that context. It provides us with that context to be creative. Just like the rules governing poetry. There are four shapes you're entitled to use and these shapes mean something and you are to use them in a certain way. There are a lot of rules governing it, but new art can still come out of that. So it becomes still memory. It's a thought. It's just a memory, even if it's a creative one. I think a lot of memory is fiction.

Kateri Akiwenzie-Damm: I know another writer from my community. We e-mail each other, and talk about working in the post-modern world. He said creative non-fiction is a dilemma since the words together are redundant and paradoxical. He started asking questions. What do they mean when they say "fiction"? "Non-fiction"? Then he got definitions out of the dictionary and sent them to me. And I started asking myself what is 'creative?' "What's fact? What's truth?" Because as soon as you start looking at definitions they raise other questions and you have to look at more definitions in order to understand the earlier definitions. He said, in the Anishnaabe language it's a different discussion because it's not so much about fiction and non-fiction, but about words and speaking. He talked about what "Anishnaabe" means and how we're supposed to act and how it's connected to speaking and our responsibility as speakers. So it was really good for me to have this internet discussion with him because he was able to help me understand what I didn't want to face. He said it's a form of oppression to have someone else name something for you.

Lee Maracle: That's right.

Kateri Akiwenzie-Damm: We might have been the ones first using this way of expressing ourselves (creative non-fiction) but we're not going to fit their definition because we don't fit in with their kind of thinking. I think that's part of the reason I was so resistant to thinking about it and to defining it because ultimately I don't find most of these definitions very helpful at all. They are only a kind of compass where you can situate yourself or situate your work, but they're not the most important aspect. Even when you use a compass you have to think "What's north? What's true north?" It's not as simple as just saying, "this is what this is and everything fits neatly into that box." To me it's a continuum and everything flows together ultimately. When I write something I don't care what anyone calls it—creative non-fiction, a story, a poem or fiction—it doesn't really matter to me. I don't quite understand why people want to do that, maybe to situate themselves. But they should not try to define the work itself using those parameters. That's a kind of colonization of the work itself.

Greg Young-Ing: The issue of categorization makes me as a publisher think of the market. Which section does Aboriginal literature go to in the bookstore? I always look in bookstores when I travel to see if they're stocking our books, and see how they're categorizing Aboriginal literature. It's done in a variety of ways. Sometimes they have a Native Studies section and they put even fiction and poetry by Aboriginal authors in that section. There are problems with that because it's implying that it's not legitimate poetry, that it doesn't deserve to be with the other poetry. And then in other stores it is put in the poetry section. But I think the Native Studies section is problematic because a novel by Lee (Maracle) or Maria Campbell) has nothing to do with a book by an academic about Aboriginal Rights. I don't know what the solution to categorization might be because they have to put books somewhere. Would an Aboriginal Literature section be appropriate, but then you can't make a section for every culture's literature. Categorization is a big problem.

Sandra Laronde: When I spoke with Sherman Alexie, he said that he hated being called a 'magical realist.' I asked him why and he said because it's a term used to categorize brown writers such as Latin American writers. I thought, that's true. It means brown writing when they say 'magical realism.'

Jeannette Armstrong: I was thinking of the pedagogy of our works. A lot of the market is aimed at universities, colleges and high schools. One of things that instructors do is they look at the work and they need to talk about it so they need to situate it. Not so much in a category but they need to say, "How do you look at this work, what do you think of this work?" So categories are sometimes a comfortable way for them to situate it. I have a problem with that because it throws everything else out. It restricts it. It's too bad how pedagogy goes like that. It says this is how this writer was thinking and it defines that piece of writing and excludes all of the other in-depth ways of approaching that work. So I think this is another thing that we need to grapple with today. We do need to have all the works approached in the most in-depth way as possible. That's one of the reasons for bringing this circle together today; to look at how instructors and teachers may have a way to approach it. Not to say how to define it, but how do you approach it. What are the different ways you can approach it, and what are the different levels of depth that you can approach these works from. I think that the creation of such a dialogue will help, not only us, but everybody else that teaches. It will help us and our new writers situate themselves in terms of the way they want to approach things. We have young writers coming up who already know how to do this, and do it really well, but get sidetracked because of the categorization.

Rasunah Marsden (Moderator): I'd like to look at some of questions that are involved with creative non-fiction. Whether or not you want to play with the definition before you actually name it, or whether you want to come up with a name. It's up to you. One of the paragraphs that we have in our kit refers to, "creative non-fiction being literary and not journalistic. The writer does not merely give information but shares an experience with the reader by telling a factual story using devices of fiction, including original research, well-crafted interpretive writing, personal discovery or experience, creative use of language, approach the subject matter, dialogue in a narrative about people who come alive." Could we refer to that in some way through the next part of the discussion?

*   *   *   *

Drew Hayden Taylor: When I first heard the term 'creative non-fiction' I was trying to think of some examples, and I too am unfamiliar with the term, but I started thinking of examples I've come across both inside and outside the Native community. The images that came to me were popular non-native novelists like Hunter S. Thompson, who advocates a type of writing he calls called 'gonzo journalism' where all the action in the story revolves around the immediate environment. There's the new journalism by Tom Wolfe called 'The Right Stuff' and then there's Truman Capote's In Cold Blood and Executioner's Song by Norman Mailer. Examples like that which are based on real events that have not been fictionalized by the writer. Mailer has gone inside the head of the main character and supplanted, or anticipated, the thoughts of the central characters. I was just looking at a flyer for Armand Garnet Ruffo's recent book, Grey Owl: Mystery of our People, and it has a quotation, "fictionalized yet based on fact." And Kateri (Akiwenzie-Damm) and I were talking about Tomson Highway's new book which everyone may be aware is a fictionalized autobiography about him and his brother—another version of that questionable term creative non-fiction. I guess I have to read now. I will read this new article I wrote:

* * * *

Drew Hayden Taylor

It Loses Something in the Translation

With the onslaught of political correctness in recent years, the term "Indian" has rapidly gone out of favour in referring to Canada's original inhabitants. Instead, a plethora of "colourful" terms, such as Native, Aboriginal, First Nations, and even Indigenous, are currently used as both adjectives and nouns in the ongoing battle to properly describe us. Even when we talk about ourselves, there is some dissension.

But the English language, now used by the vast majority of Native people, and the words we have chosen for self description in these more enlightened times, are no better than "Indian," that ubiquitous "sub-continent" term from by-gone days. In fact, many find the numerous Aboriginal-related terms' correctness suspect and their usage questionable. Unfortunately, it can be confusing being an English-speaking First Nations person.

The term First Nations, to me, is a political phrase, often used to describe what used to be called a reserve. For instance, I come from the Curve Lake First Nation. But personally, I am a little uncomfortable being called a First Nations person because I do not consider myself a political term. Therefore to say I am First Nations limits me to a strictly political nature or definition. And who wants that? Cynics will argue that everything is political. Especially being Native in Canada. But I would still rather be a person than a political definition. Call me a rebel if you will.

The other term of questionable description is the familiar expression

"Aboriginal." Deconstructing the word, the prefix "ab," used in such other well-known words as abominable (as in the abominable snowman), abhorrent, absurd, abysmal, abnormal, abscess, abase, abject, to name a few, all have a negative connotation. They all seem to denote a certain pessimistic designation or flavour to what ever is being discussing. Thus, being an Aboriginal is not a very flattering term. But it does beg the question "Could the Inuit of the Arctic be called the Aboriginal snowmen?"

Taking this issue a bit further, I was once sitting in the office of the Native Student Coordinator for a large university. I accidentally overheard the coordinator talking on the phone with a new student that was interested in coming in for a chat. I heard a familiar phrase being issued by this keeper of the office: "Are you of Native descent?" The immediate image in my mind was of a Native person taking an escalator to the basement. Descent makes me think of descending. Therefore, being of Native descent is a step downwards. I think we should take command of this language that has taken command of us; I prefer to think of myself as being of Native ascent. I think others should too. I, as well as our people, want to go up in the world, not down.

Above and beyond personal definitions of our culture, the intermingling of Native and non-Native realities, as often occurs through English usage, never fails to amaze me. Several times a year I get invited to various Native Awareness Weeks across the country, usually at universities (no doubt with descending Native students). The irony of the term "awareness" occurred to me one day as I was driving through a small town on my way to such an event. A large banner across the main street alerted the residents that this was also Cancer Awareness Week. In another town I visited recently it was Aids Awareness Week. Still others advertised Diabetes Awareness Week.

And here I was going to Native Awareness Week. Perhaps, with enough money and research, there will be no more need for these Awareness Weeks and these evil scourges will officially be wiped out for ever. My donation is in the mail.

There also seems to be a noticeable gulf in the interpretations of certain words in both cultures. The most obvious to me occurred during the editing of a new book I had coming out. The publisher wrote some promo material and asked me to proof it. I read it over several times but found myself concerned with a certain passage—one word, in fact—that I felt was misleading and could possibly be construed as inappropriate.

I argued with the publisher for several minutes before the misunderstanding became quite evident. The line itself read "...big questions of heritage, family, cultural context and personal identity are ruthlessly stripped of their traditional meanings and become so much useless, embarrassing roadkill on the highway of life."

It was the word "traditional" that I felt was both misleading and inappropriate. I was reading the word from a specifically Native perspective, and taking that into account, the quote sounds somewhat harsh and provocative. Judge for yourself. But the publisher was using the term "traditional" in the context of what is generally believed or accepted. Once we both realized this, we merely changed "traditional" to "conventional," and both went away happy little literary people.

English has been with Native people for just a few centuries now. And it's no secret there has always been a communication problem in one form or another. On the cusp of the millennium, the battle still continues.

* * * *

Sandra Laronde: In your writing is there something about the process of writing?

Drew Hayden Taylor: It depends. I just get an idea and I think, "what's interesting about this idea?" "What's a new way to look at it, a way to reinterpret it?" Sometimes it's the process of writing. Sometimes it's autobiographical. Being who I am. Being where I am. What I'm doing. Sometimes it's political, social, cultural, artistic. I mean there's no rhyme or reason. I'm a storyteller, that's all.

Lee Maracle: I just want to tell you this story since we were talking about not being all that familiar with the culture. I was working at a show with a group of Elders who came from a community that was never christianized. They split off from the larger group because they didn't want to be christianized and they had a special kind of agreement with the Presbyterian Church which guaranteed that they didn't have to become christians without the consent of the entire extended family. They had this weird complex about becoming christian, so they have a different history. They were talking about a process called *mizokopapiwin*, which means, "go around in circles and look for something that is cherished yet hidden." There is a way to do that and each person is charged with the responsibility of finding a new perspective. And they'll play with it until what's hidden and cherished becomes known to them.

It's a process of discovery and it's a process of conflict resolution. This is how they do it and go through this process. It has a number of facilitators that go with it to make sure that everyone looks at it in a different way. And they first establish the way they are looking at it and then they go into council again and everyone comes up with a new way of looking at it. They keep doing this until something shows itself to them. Then they identify it as the new thing that's cherished and hidden. Thus a consensus is achieved. I was thinking it was such a mature form of play. That's why the other night I was talking to Drew (Hayden Taylor) and said, "Drew, you're so Ojibway," because you do exactly what this process is all about. So futuristic in a way and it has to do with taking command of this language and being brave in the reshaping of it, the taking charge of it and taking into a different place. Taking it to somewhere in the past so that we can go somewhere in the future. I'm not in a hurry to name things. But the taking command of language is, I think, what we're all doing right now. And playing with it is something we've been doing for a little while. I think that we could probably do it for another generation without feeling compelled to name it. Although I think there's power in naming, but there's also closure. We don't want to close the door on someone that's coming behind us that will open it wider for us. We're just sort of playing around with this English.

Dorothy Christian (Observer): Maria, I'd like you to talk more about stories you've been taught as a storyteller and the discipline that you must exercise in doing those stories as opposed to your own stories. How are you with respect to the rules that you have been told by your Elders in terms of the stories that are in your culture? And yet you still do the creative non-fiction that a lot of us are playing around with out there.

Maria Campbell: I know that from my own personal experience as a writer that for the longest time I couldn't get out of the Oral Tradition rules. And I did have all of this stuff that I wanted to put down on paper. I felt like I had all these other things in me all trying to talk at once and I couldn't sort through it. The ones that wanted to talk were much more powerful than I was. That only changed in the last year so that I've been able to look at the creative writing, the poetry and the short stories, and start to make changes when I edit it.

There are different kinds of rules than English. When the Elders teach you how to do something, it's like if you're learning to do a ceremony. If you make a mistake there are consequences. So with some of those stories, there are consequences. So you could get into serious trouble when you are learning them. You make sure you do them right. But then it depends on what stories you're learning. We have in Cree a whole group of names that say what kind of storyteller you are. Although no one says it in the community, everybody knows what kind of stories you tell. You wouldn't go and tell a different kind of story because you wouldn't know how. But if you did try it, then the people would help you because they'd think you were trying to learn. I guess in English it's called genre, but I don't even know if you can compare.

I'd like to ask Jeannette this, "Can you compare traditional stories to things that you say in English?" Because the laws are in there so you have to be really precise. Some of them you can't translate at all. You have to speak them and only in that language. Just translating them you can't find an English word that will have the same meaning.

Jeannette Armstrong: We were discussing that issue in our language class with the people who are fluent speakers of the high language of the Okanagan. One of the things we do know is that the codification in our stories are contained in very clear symbols. Maybe in other traditions they might be the same. When you are speaking about a specific symbol, or a metaphor, that is a reference point to a number of other things, which, in the cultural context, are already known. For instance, if we were to say in English, "the road or the trail," the symbol of the trail isn't just about a path that people walk but also a pathway of life. So symbolically there are a number of things like that and we don't have to say.

One really important aspect of language and translation and story—and this is where the appropriation issue comes in—is that people need to be clear if they are writing from their cultures that they are not messing up in terms of that really clear pathway. And that's done. That's done even by people who are knowledgeable in the language and the culture. So that they're not mixing and matching like some New Ager. To a large extent because of the disappearance of our languages we culturally need to put some clear thought to it.

There's also the aspect of esoteric knowledge. Knowledge that isn't meant for anyone else except practitioners. That's one of the reasons why there were societies, there were clans that kept esoteric knowledge. That didn't mean we could not use the symbolism. In order to look at it from a story context and with the depth of meaning, I think there needs to be some clear thought put toward how traditional stories and traditional words are used. Particularly information that can be misrepresented outside. So it's always good to check with people who are knowledgeable, who are interpreters, in the culture.

Lee Maracle: I just want to add to that from my understanding of the Salish Raven stories, which are stories of transformation and change. Those are the stories in which we are given a framework to tell and then you create a context yourself. So it's actually a creative process, you actually make it up. A new story out of an old story. Those are the ones that I play with in my writing because everyone's entitled to do that. Those are the ones that change house-to-house, place-to-place. And then you have these sociological stories which the grandmas who run the house have. And you don't play with those stories without permission from the matriarchs who run the household. Then there are the clan stories. There is a huge, complex process in getting access to a clan story, an old story, a visionary story or a bear story. And then it moves along to the esoteric, or the medicine stories, and those are the ones that have a place in our world that hasn't anything to do with storytelling. Those are things that we don't play with at all. There's a lot of governance regarding them. We haven't had the opportunity to really have a look at that in the modern context and take the governance of all those things. It's the same as the Raven stories, I mean there are rules, governance around these stories, directions they're supposed to go.

Jeannette Armstrong: I published a story in the All My Relations collection that was called "This is a Story." It's a contemporary story of *Kyote* coming across the Grand Coulee Dam. Now that's a contemporary story, in terms of him coming back to life, waking up and finding Grand Coulee Dam and that all the swallows (colonizers) have taken over everything. In that story the structure has to be very clear and consistent and the reference points back to the original story when he first broke the dam. So the reference point and the way *Kyote* acts and what he does, all the different things that *Kyote* is known for is strictly adhered to in the story.

Maria Campbell: Yeah, you have to go back and forth a lot. It's the same for us so you have to do another kind of translation for yourself when you are working like that.

Lee Maracle: I want to talk about that cultural preservation. First of all, preservation is to pickle something, to save it for later. Culture is dynamic. We conduct ourselves within it. We connect with it. I just want to jump off with what Jeannette (Armstrong) was saying because in my tradition an act is committed to show something. For Salish people we are here on this earth to discover consequence. That's what I'm here for. There's no other purpose in my being here. I'm here to learn consequences and go back and chat with my ancestors and see what we can make of the Spirit World, that world that exists forever. So I am directed to go to the bottom of the sea, in terms of achieving depth. That's the process. We're to achieve depth. You go through lovely little layers of green to get to this ceremonial black. We're not as secure in this light. This light blinds.

As I understand it, as Salish beings, we actually see more clearly in total dark. It's comfortable. And then you come to understanding. The first whole part of my novel <u>Ravensong</u> is that black. All that's left to understand is the arc of the bridge between the main character and white people. The whole purpose of that book is on that arc, in the discovery of it. What I learned from writing that book is that it's not at all what's on the arc, it's about those fish jumping up whenever she looks over the bridge. So Raven comes into light, beaming at some point, and keeps getting this character to look down into the water. She doesn't actually see anything there because I'm not looking there. The author's looking there. The author wants you to know about this arc. Well out of it came two things. The writing of the book redirected the book, culturally, and changed my perspective, which is the objective of understanding consequence.

In that way, the past serves the future and the moment and what you wrestle with. Then you direct yourself. Connect yourself to your past and direct yourself in the future. That's my purpose for being in this world. It's what I try to do in my life and writing is a moment in my life.

Maria Campbell: I think about my own people's language, I learned both of them. Then I married a Saulteau man and learned to speak his language and my grandson, who's twenty-five, learned when I taught him stories in both my languages. Some of the things that have been given to me by my Saulteau Grandmother-in-law, I can't really use. They're not mine, even if I speak the language and I can understand them. But growing up with the two languages was really difficult. In my own community, I'm accused sometimes, mostly by political people, that I'm too much Cree. "Well you're not really Métis, you're Cree." And then I go to the Cree they say, "You're too Métis." And I am, I'm more Cree than I am Métis. I'm Métis but I'm more Cree. So on one hand I'm more Cree than Métis, Cree is my first language. Talk about cultural identity.

Kateri Akiwenzie Damm: That's interesting because I don't always know. That's something that a lot of writers, especially these days, struggle with because we may not have had all of the instruction in traditional storytelling to know what those rules are. It becomes very difficult to find your way through that and not silence yourself because that's the other direction you can go. It can become so difficult that you don't want to tell the stories that you have. I just wanted to raise that because it pops up every once in while for me and I get nervous about the way I'm trying to tell a story. On the other hand I have to. I don't know how else to express myself a lot of the time. It's always a dilemma for me. I try to come from a place of truth and I feel an obligation to share, because I don't think knowledge should be hoarded and kept to one's self. I feel pulled in all different directions trying to express myself as person who does have some cultural knowledge and is learning. I'm thirty-four years old and I'm still learning. I feel like an infant in terms of my knowledge. So for me it's a huge dilemma. I tread carefully. It's a journey I believe is connected to spiritual growth and development. I know that there are a lot of other young artists who have the same questions and difficulties trying to balance all that out. You might come from several different backgrounds and have certain knowledge of each one, but maybe they are not complete. No one is complete and yet you are a complete person living your life in a certain way.

Maria Campbell: One of my teachers told me that the most important thing is to speak the language. It's one of the things I feel so fortunate about. But if you can't speak the language the most important thing is to respect. If you have a real respect for your own gift and if you respect people and traditions, then your instinct will tell you what to do. Sandra (Laronde) was talking about memory in your body, those things that tell you to be careful when you are doing something. I call it the grandmother in you. It tells you tread carefully even if you don't think about it. You run into trouble if you don't respect that gift. When I think back to when I was much younger and I didn't take it seriously, didn't respect it, I got into trouble. If you don't respect that in yourself, your voice, that spirit that's there, then you don't have any direction.

Lee Maracle: But that's a part of life.

Maria Campbell: I know, but it warns you. You know that you have to careful.

Sandra Laronde: Sometimes a voice tells me, "I can't do this." I mean it's not even a little "no" inside. It's a big "no." I just realize, that, "it's not my boundary to break." This boundary will be pushed, but it's not mine to push. I realize that. It feels really good to heed that voice, it feels like you grow a little inside.

Jeannette Armstrong: Then you can be really creative. You can figure out how to really have impact and what needs to be said, but not be invasive in those areas that are sacred, where the esoteric or cultural boundary might be. So you respect that in the creativity around that, but still do what needs to be done in terms of the power of the story. That's creativity.

* * * *

Sandra Laronde: I'm just going to read an excerpt from a piece that I've been creating called *"N'Daki Menan."* I wanted to play with the idea that in the forest there are many similarities to society. The young ones growing up need shade from too much light or they do what is called suckering. They grow all over the place because they don't have a pathway to grow towards the light. I wanted to play with the imagery in the forest and liken it to society. When they go in and cut the old ones down, it's like people and what they do with Elders. They put them away someplace so they can't be seen. It's all about new growth, and tree farming. There's a serious manipulation of an ecosystem without realizing the bio-diversity that a forest or a society needs to survive.

Where I come from in Temagami, a third of the ancient white pine left in the entire world is there. There are ancient trees that are hundreds of years old. That's important to me, to somehow put the land of Temagami in this piece, and to show how we as Teme-Augama-Anishnaabe are a testimony to the deep humanness and the principle of sharing and co-existence in which our people are culturally thousands of years old.

(Stands up and performs the following:)

* * * *

SANDRA LARONDE

"N' DAKI MENAN"

EXCERPT FROM WORK IN PROGRESS

My brother jumps. I hope he changes into a bird and flies away because
I know that all he's really looking for is a nest. Can't you just see his little
bird feet tickling some big old tree? Tickle, tickle, tickle! I'll be that tree,
laughing inside rough bark and tickling him with my tender needles. His
tears will flood out of his mouth and form liquid golden words and there
he'll live in the spring that he deserves to touch. But in this long winter
he's living right now, I am the snow that keeps him warm. How can I
grow when chains chew my brother's flesh and mark my time when I am
fallen? Breathe in my limbs. You coax sap with your sweet sun. But I
freeze. Should I grow? Should I reap life into your air? Slow. Oh my silent
sky, I am marked. I am gashed. I am chained to time. I cannot but exhale
and you cannot but breathe me in. I drink you in. I grow into your arms
and die. Oh my love, my love, my sky.

* * * *

Greg Young-Ing: There are issues that I've been writing about in a paper that I'm currently doing for my Masters in Publishing degree at Simon Fraser University. It's called, "Understanding People On Their Own Terms: A Rationale for an Aboriginal Style Guide." I started to realize that it is a creative non-fiction piece in itself, but at the same time I'm doing it to establish editorial guidelines for working with Aboriginal material. I'll just read a couple of excerpts from it.

* * * *

GREG YOUNG-ING

"UNDERSTANDING PEOPLE ON THEIR OWN TERMS:
A RATIONALE FOR AN ABORIGINAL STYLE GUIDE"

EXCERPT FROM WORK IN PROGRESS

There are various ways in which Aboriginal cultural integrity is not respected in the writing and publishing process. Among the most common are as follows:

1) Aboriginal intellectual property is written down incorrectly and/or misinterpreted through European-based cultural perspectives;

2) Aboriginal intellectual property is claimed by "authors" who are re-telling and/or transcribing previously existing intellectual heritage;

3) Aspects of Aboriginal culture that are "owned" by (i.e., are the intellectual property of) particular Elders, families or clans are appropriated (i.e., told without permission and/or claimed by authors);

4) Aspects of Aboriginal culture that have specific internal regulations associated with their use (i.e., they can only be told by certain people, in certain ceremonies and/or at certain times of the year) have those regulations broken;

5) Traditional stories, legends, ceremonies, dances and/or objects such as masks, that are deemed as sacred and not intended for public domain, are appropriated and presented in books.

Awareness that these practices breach Aboriginal cultural protocol, and the extent to which they constitute severe offences within Aboriginal cultural confines, is lacking among the Canadian public and this is often reflected in the publishing industry.

Another common error found in literature is referring to Aboriginal Peoples in the past tense. In the book <u>First People, First Voices</u>, edited by Penny Petrone in 1983, the opening paragraph states, "From ancient times the Indians have **lived** in the lands now known as Canada... They **fed** and clothed themselves off the usually bountiful land, **lived** in harmony with the Great Spirit... They also **sang** songs, **told** stories, and **passed** traditions on by word of mouth through succeeding generations." (emphasis added)

Apart from the stereotypical view of Aboriginal Peoples portrayed in this text, it contains another major problem commonly found in writing about Aboriginal Peoples; namely, it speaks of them in the past tense. Referring to Aboriginal Peoples in the past tense has the following implications that are considered inappropriate and offensive to many Aboriginal Peoples:

• that they no longer exist as distinct cultures in a ongoing continuum through the generations tracing back to their ancient ancestors;

• that they no longer practice such cultural activities as traditional storytelling, traditional songs and religious beliefs (as per the above quote); and, thus,

• that contemporary Aboriginal Peoples have been assimilated into mainstream Canadian society to the point that they no longer identify with their ancestors, or that Aboriginal cultures have been fundamentally altered or undermined through colonization.

Indeed, as has been discussed previously, some of these implications are cornerstones of the mainstream perception of Aboriginal Peoples. This is perhaps why the "past tense" is still used often in written material on Aboriginal Peoples, particularly within the disciplines of anthropology, archaeology and art history.

* * * *

Maria Campbell: I'll read from the play "Negotiations." What I did when I started to work on the play was that I started to work on the scenarios. I talked to different people and I asked, "What would you say in this situation?"

* * * *

MARIA CAMPBELL

"NEGOTIATIONS"

EXCERPT FROM WORK IN PROGRESS

(In a man's voice:)

We used to come to this river every spring to trap rats, me and the old mans. We came with a team of horses and we'd bring all our traps, a rifle and some grub. We make our camp right here. That was a long time ago. Damn near seventy years ago, I was about six years old when I started coming with them. The old mans would make the camp and me I had to look for *Waskwayimitosah*, that's birch trees. I never have to go far... just over there. By golly there's still lots of them. See, in the morning the old mans, they make a *mutootsan*. And me, I have to kill a young dog, clean it and cook it. When the old mans they finish the *mutootsan*, I bring the dog soup and they make prayers on it then we eat it. When we're done we all go to the bush and the old men would cut some saplings to make a frame for canoes. I'd show them the birch trees and the old men would take the bark off them. And me, I'd have to pick a couple of pails of *pikoo*, you know, what hees call spruce gum! And I gots to boil it up. They used that gum for glue and boy he sure works good too. We make a couple of canoes out of that bark. We have a *mutootsan* and dog feast. 'Cause *Waskwayimitosah*, he's special and we have to give thanks for using him. When we're finished trapping, bout a couple weeks, sometimes longer, we'd come back here and the old mans they have a pipe and make some more prayers. Then we burn them canoes with tobacco...

(Now a woman's voice:)

My grandmother and my great grandmother were both midwives. You could probably go back further because mother always said women in my family have always birthed the babies and buried the dead. That's hard work you know. I was never strong that way. Remember that meadow across from the old house, they call it Bergen's meadow. Well it used to be called *oomisimahoo pasquahoo*, but that was a long time ago, before the white people took over. They just took over, you know. Never even asked us or said excuse me. I remember that. Well that meadow was where the old women picked the medicine they used for midwifery. That tall, blue flower, that was the main one. It was used for stopping hemorrhages. A lot of women would have died if we didn't have that flower. And all over, at the edge of those trees in the meadow, that's where the afterbirth and those things were buried. Old women used to bury it with tobacco. They were really careful. I used to help my grandmother carry stuff over there and I'd dig the hole for her. She said everybody whose afterbirth was buried here would always come back to this land because a part of their *awchak* was here. And such nice flowers and trees grew there. And the medicine, it grew the best on the places where we buried that stuff. Grandmother used to say afterbirth is medicine. And it was true, too.

* * * *

Maria Campbell: This first excerpt was from my cousin. I told him to imagine what he would want to say if he was at the negotiations table speaking on what was happening to his land. If he was allowed to speak he said, "I'd like to talk about a river." He told me that this was an actual story of his. And then I talked to the old lady, I said to imagine that all these things are happening on your land, what would you want to say. So I gave her the section where I wanted to hear her voice.

* * * *

Kateri Akiwenzie-Damm: I'm still learning how to tell this story so this is more of a first go at it.

* * * *

KATERI AKIWENZIE-DAMM

NANABUSH AT THE SYDNEY AIRPORT

Nanabush is walking through Sydney Airport. She has just returned to Sydney from visiting friends in Broome and Alice Springs and is waiting for her flight to Aotearoa. She is wandering through shops looking at surfer gear and pens with cartoon koala bears and kangaroos splattered across them. She picks out a couple of baseball caps with surfing logos to give away to friends.

Nanabush had come to Sydney weeks earlier to attend an international gathering of Indigenous tricksters. Oh sure, it was called the Festival of something-or-other but she, Maui, Coyote, Fox, Raven, the Featherfoots… all the gang had been there. It had been especially good to see Maui again. Hard case, that one! She never knew who he'd be when she met him again. One time a heartbreaker, the next…? And she never knew what he'd do.

"Nah, you just never know with that one," she thinks, smiling. This time, that trickster Maui showed as the heartbreaker's brother, also known as Maui. Tricky all right!

"The whole family is Maui, come to think of it," thinks Nanabush. "Maui the first, Maui the middle, Maui the edge. Maui, Maui, Maui." Picking out the trickster Maui from those brothers was a trick in itself. Heartbreaker Maui had a knack for keeping her off balance so she almost always felt like she was walking against the current or moving against the forces of gravity when she was in his territory. But all in all, she was kind of proud of how she was able to survive and thrive there on the other side of the world where winter was summer and today is tomorrow and the water runs down the drain in the opposite direction. Damn proud. "One of my best tricks," she boasted.

Truth is Nanabush adores the Maui family. Even before she'd fallen in love with the Heartbreaker Maui, she'd loved them. "It's that trickster outcast thang they've got happening," she reckons. "Maui—James Dean of the trickster world!" Well, she always had been attracted to rebels with supernatural powers. Oh Maui. Maui! The way he hooked that fish and created land! *Weeshitau-ta-hauw!* Now, THAT was a *Manitou* after her own heart, hey. Was it any wonder she'd fallen for him.?

But, he'd thrown her heart back like fish guts into the ocean.

Maybe his ancient failure with *Hine-nui-te-po* made him *porangi, hoha*, needing to pluck out the heart of a goddess and leave her for dead. After all, what trickster-hero in his right mind would let one so fine as Nanabush get away? He deserves to be an outcast then. Nanabush grins. "Because you are a good strong loving trickster hero goddess and you don't need any of his I-am-an-island supernatural loverboy trickster shit. You are a good strong loving trickster hero. You are a good…"

Nanabush walks outside repeating the chant under her breath. It is a sunny and warm October day Down Under. She sits on a bench just outside the terminal door and watches the smokers puffing and pulling in their cheeks on the platform across the road. Not one of them seems to be praying. Wasting that perfectly good tobacco she sniffs self-righteously.*Shawganosh-nee-nahow!*

Disgusted, she stands and walks to the terminal doors. She likes the way the doors open on their own. Good majik that, she thinks. Wonder who got the idea and gave it to these humans? Probably Raven. That Raven, he's just crazy enough to think of a way to have doors open on their own. And what a big blabbermouth that one is too. Always squawking and carrying on. Loves the sound of his own voice that one. Not like Nanabush. Nanabush is demure.

Nanabush is walking through Sydney airport. She stops at a shop and is staring at a rack of gum and chocolates and candies. Lollies, they call 'em here, eh. She looks at the clock and yawns in that way Nanabush is inclined to do to cover her own boredom and impatience. She'd go through security and customs soon. Meanwhile...yawn. Gum. Good idea. She pats her pockets looking for change...

Shit!

Ohmigawddesself. Shit. Shit. Damn. Shit.

There in her very own jacket pocket is the joint that Maui the Third had handed her that morning as he and his party left for the airport. She'd stuck it in her pocket and totally forgotten about it until now. Now, damn you Maui, when she's standing in the middle of a busy airport full of cameras and security guards. Now, when she's about to go through security and customs.

Nanabush is walking through the Sydney airport.

Well, not so much walking as skulking, pacing, slinking through. Suddenly there is a security guard. Every few steps. Not to mention those men and women who look far too normal and disinterested in her to be anything but narcs.

Nanabush is walking through the airport thinking really hard. Thinking really hard and yawing. Yawning as Nanabush is inclined to do when she envisions getting busted.

Nanabush is walking and walking and thinking and thinking and yawning and yawning and trying hard not to look like someone trying hard not to look like she has drugs in her pocket. Eheh, she is trying very hard indeed to look like someone not looking suspicious.

Just then Nanabush has a thought. Oh clever Nanabush. She smiles and walks outside telling herself how clever, how good and strong she is. No, she doesn't exactly walk. She feels lighter than before she had thought this clever thought. So she *glides* outside the terminal building, crosses the road to the platform and smiles her dazzling Nanabush smile at the other smokers. Filled with self-assurance she marches to the smoking area and finds an isolated spot behind a pillar. She sits on the concrete tile and leans back against the cold pillar behind her. She takes the joint from her pocket.

Sunlight falls across her face. She can see people on the ground below her, crossing from the parking lot to the arrivals entrance. Not one of them looks up. Cool.

She flicks her lighter.

Careful now, she holds the end of the tube of illicit substance like a rollie, just in case anyone is looking.

She wraps her lips around it, holding it between her fingers, puts a flame to the end and pulls her cheeks in. AAH. She puffs her cheeks in and out like any other smoker.

Mmm.

Yes, that was a very clever thought indeed.

Moments later Nanabush is walking through Sydney airport.

Next step, customs and security. Now the real trick. The trick worthy of a consummate trickster hero like herself. <u>Do not in any way appear to be stoned</u>. She enters the customs area, fills out a declaration, takes a deep breath, looks as sober as a New World missionary and lines up.

"Canada." "New Zealand." "One month." "No." She suppresses smiling her dazzling Nanabush smile. Even that might seem suspicious. She thinks of the smoke and wonders if she's standing downwind from the customs agent.

The agent barely looks up, puts his mark on her declaration then pushes it back at her. At the next desk, she hands it to the next agent who hands it back and waves her through.

Nanabush is walking through Sydney airport security.

She strolls, emptying her pockets of keys and change so as not to set off any alarms. "Through security and I'm free."

She passes through security, no problem.

Nanabush walks into the women's washroom. As she's peeing she laughs at Maui. As she buttons her pants and tucks in her shirt she tells herself how clever she is. Australian security is no match for Nanabush!.

With an hour to go before the flight leaves Nanabush is walking through the Sydney.airport. She sashays into a shop smiling her dazzling Nanabush smile. She buys an apple then struts and slides and glides to a seat across from her gate.

She notices an obviously love struck young man a few rows over, staring at her. She looks at him then looks away, tilting her head and batting her eyes just like Princess Di but only sexier because after all, she is

Nanabush. A trickster hero goddess diva who loved the Heartbreaker Maui and not some mere mortal princess with an eating disorder and big eared husband.

"This is a pre-boarding announcement for passengers."

Nanabush rises and saunters toward the women's washroom. Men stare. Their jaws hit the floor. Their eyes pop from their sockets. Her hips swish and sway. She smiles her dazzling Nanabush smile, pulls open the door and steps inside. She winks at herself with not bloodshot eyes. Not stoned looking eyes. "No one knows" she tells herself again, shaking her head and laughing at her trick. "For nearly two hours I've tricked them all. They are no match for me. For I am Nanabush and I am the most clever trickster hero of them all!"

She struts, saunters, sashays and shimmies from the mirror to the bathroom stall.

She looks down.

"Whaaaa!!"

Her zipper is wide open and the corner of her shirt is poking out like some poor girls strap-on. Like a little white cotton penis poking out between the teeth of her zipper.

"Nanabush," she laughs, "You are a good strong loving crazy trickster fool."

And she smiles that dazzling Nanabush smile.

* * * *

Rasunah Marsden (Moderator): Just looking at the readings, it's pretty obvious that nobody wants to stick to any particular style or structure. There are mixtures of poetry, prose, commentary and all kinds of things we consider Indigenous creative non-fiction to be. One of the more common forms that are accessible to the vanguard are what I call identity pieces or forms of commentary which defy labels like political commentary or social commentary. One of the commentaries that I wanted to read an excerpt from is called "Repatriation of a Soul". This is the last section.

*   *   *   *

Rasunah Marsden

"Repatriation of a Soul"

an Excerpt

My father was raised on a reserve .

We usually don't talk about these things. He comes from the generation that was silenced. He has not said he was not proud to be of Indigenous descent. He has felt validated that his child has understood the decisions he made to survive and the decisions he made as a father and he has been accorded the honour he deserved. He came from the generation of Indigenous children whose language was slapped out of their faces. There is great difference between thinking there is something wrong with your blood and the understanding that you have done what you could do to survive, and that you have struggled to reach a point of success in your life where you can taste a simple enjoyment in life which no one should be denied. For him, who recently had a heart attack, it is almost too late to feel this, but just the taste is worth his whole life. This is from a man for whom the nobility of the soul was an automatic knowledge which he did not have to learn from books.

I was not raised on a reserve.

So in the first sense returning to Indian country, which is everywhere there are Native people, I did not want to feel well for who I was, simply because I could not have suffered the things that my ancestors suffered. At first you can feel this as a tangible block that makes you think you are not acceptable anywhere. For instance, I did not fight that history of battles and I was not a political person. So you have the idea that you are not Indian enough in some way for not knowing that history of how that marginalization was accomplished. What works against this is inner knowledge that you never, though you were trained in Anglo-western ways, believed that those ways were the best or only ways.

In the second sense, repatriation of the soul, the feeling of being at home, is blocked through the ignorance that you can not only undeniably feel it or spend your life feeling it. And yet another part of you understands that the traditional practices, the cornerstones of fasting and wisdom of stories which speak of the foundations of Native world-views, are precisely the elements which your soul responds to as being the strength and wisdom of the people. At the same time it is encouraging that people who believe in the humanity of the soul will recognize each other, without prejudice. This is a very tall order which life's difficulties sometimes cause us to ignore.

As one who follows my inner guidance as well as I am able, it is with thankfulness that I value the inborn tendency to do so because of what is Indigenous in my blood for these are peoples who have been abused. To be able to stand as a human being despite that history of abuse makes the sense of freedom which is felt as a birthright, sweeter than what a person from a colonizing culture, in coming to terms with ones' own spiritual journey, could ever feel. This is like saying that two people need to reach the top of the same mountain but one of them, having been forced to be subservient, carries the other on his back. They both reach the top and stand on it. One of them has one less burden to carry. The one who did not have that burden feels no different, but the other's feeling of freedom is that much greater, that much sweeter.

*   *   *   *

LEE MARACLE

MEMORY SERVES

We are called upon to remember when humans give breath to life, give voice to their perception of life, this is a sacred act. They are taking an event which has already been committed and they are remembering or reconstructing it.

Memory serves in a society governed first by spirit to spirit relationships to all beings.

Memory serves. To remember is first directional.

We remember events, acts committed, because we are all aware that those acts, having already ended, are dismembered, gone forever.

We remember consciously because we wish to achieve a new direction, secure an old direction or mark the path travelled so that others may find it easier to follow. This is what governs our lives and shapes our oracy. It is also the governor of Native literacy.

Creative non-fiction does not exist outside the original foundations handed to us by our ancestors, our ceremony, our laws and our relationship to creation.

Memory serves. In our culture we re-member hundreds of thousands of relationships, to wind, to flora, to fauna, to humans, to the dead, the star world, sky world, sea world. Everything from the humble snow flea on a glacier, to the glacial age is remembered for today and for tomorrow. There is no time differentiation in the conjuring of memory.

Future is a remembered thing the very moment I give voice inside my mind to the imagined participation in tomorrow.

Re-membering takes place in the imagination. The moment the act is over it is dismembered. The reconstruction of the images surrounding it takes place in our imagination. Depending on the place and perspective of the viewer, the images take on meaning. The place and perception of the viewer influences the direction of the imagined events and this colours the reconstruction of memory.

For this reason memory can betray the spiritual desire of the remembered. If the words you choose take on a challenging direction when what is desired is re-connection, you will conjure memory in one way and your response to your own conjuring will betray your long distance desire.

I watch my daughter, hear her rise. She marches back and forth in front of me. The words tumble out, razor-sharp and full of insult. Her thin arms punctuate every sentence which splits the breath between us. Her eyes flash fire. I did not accept what she says. In my shock I retreat to an old game I play. Watch the speaker, grocery list her moves, turn my listening volume down low, just record what you see. Try not to listen. Try hard to remain aloof and amuse myself with the activity I am committing to memory.

Later in my room, I am about to indulge in another old habit, reconstruct the insult and persuade myself that it is not about me being offended but rather about the other being the offender. I hesitate. This is my daughter after all. Some little soft voice whispered inside my mind, "Remember to what end?" That question rolled about for a long time.

I had no way to answer it and for the first time since I was a child I was forced to take my own advice. I picked up the stone on my dresser and asked this old grandfather to help me answer the question, "to what end?"

Sleep came as it does when life presents more agitation for my soul than I necessarily desired. Stone sang as he does:

I carry your bones now that I am gone. These bones that are stones, laying cream white in my apron. I walk carefully not to make any sudden moves so as not to jar you or add any new song to them. I want only the pure sounds of you and me which we were waiting for you to echo back to me on those long nights when alone and night makes doubtful friends.

Me wondering, am I going the right way? Did I choose words of the sacred, carefully uphold the day? I still miss you after all this time. We chose to leave that first time. I remember that day as I stare at your bones and the stones full of small weird clues.

Bread crumb trails we say today.

The earth wept a torrential rain that day, greening our leaving. We didn't want anyone to know why we left. It was our first secret. A secret knowing upon us in the wake of our first change. This overwhelming desire to appease the families, the birthlight inside our bellies was going mad inside our stomachs. Running around and trying to understand and appreciate what they saw us do.

My body wrenched. Every piece of me wanted to run in all directions like the pains in my belly whenever I remember the images that led to our leaving.

We gathered our bones together, you and I.

We reached inside the stone memory of our bodies for song, for depth, for knowing and pulled on every part of our lives for future.

We sang.

We wept with earth as we conjured the plan to leave these holes that you shaped, without taking you with us.

We executed the plan, my sisters and I.

Despite agreement by each and every one of us on the new journey we embarked upon. I still ache from it.

We've earned every dead one except those with no one to care for them.

I burnt you, my branch.

I collected your ash, your bone fragments.

Wrapped you in cedar and placed you so gently in my apron.

This pillar of smoke you made burning between bits and pieces of our lives rose majestic as you saluted me before we left.

Being can be treacherous. Good intentions and love are not enough. Colourful whispers awed by the fire you made in the remembering.

We must have law and discipline, I murmured, finishing the thought and a clear path to embrace it was added to deepen it, and the rush of tears was so great we nearly put out the fire.

*   *   *   *

Lee Maracle: That's from a piece of our history.

* * * *

Jeannette Armstrong: Scott Momaday published his essay, "The Man Made of Words" in the seventies in <u>The Remembered Earth</u>. For those of you looking for something to read, this essay was a turning point in my life. I was in university at the time, studying creative writing and literature. I had no access to anything that was Indigenous that I could remember except for Maria Campbell and a few others. So this is the piece that gave me insight. The essay itself is about Oral Tradition. It's the way that he frames this piece in his talk about his process of writing.

The central idea of that essay, and the bringing forward out of racial memory, is what this work was organized from. It's in his words, when he creates this essay he brings forth this woman, this grandmother. For he makes her a grandmother of 137 years ago as well as his own voice that's speaking. It's not really an identity piece in that way or a personalized piece. After reading that essay I attempted to put together something that turned out to be a poem which I later did as a performance piece. It's published in my book <u>Breathtracks</u> and it's called "World Renewal Song." I imagined me and the grandmother and imagined this woman so this isn't actually identity. In a metaphorical sense it is all Okanagan women who have gone, in our tradition, on a vision quest to renew their world and renew their promise. In terms of non-fiction it's also speaking about a real personal experience. I perform this piece as a personal "song of self." In Okanagan we call it *sqilmxqin*. It's about me, but also about the universal "me" or "spirit me."So this is actually a song, a song for the renewal of the world, but I can't sing it without doing the whole piece.

* * * *

JEANNETTE ARMSTRONG

"WORLD RENEWAL SONG"

Nothing was good
Winds blew
and grasses died

I thought I was pitied
So I longed
for a Whole Time Song
I danced for it
in deerskins

I made thought with paint
in red lines
from left finger to shoulder

I silent
sitting by dying
grasses
began hearing
at dawn

A new fire is lighted
The finished world is here
formed in mind patches...

*   *   *   *

Jeannette Armstrong: We have a racial memory. Those things that our people cherish. We can't claim them. We have to respect them. We can find a way to bring them through when we don't have all the pieces or some of them have been forgotten or clouded by memory, or fragmented because we've been fragmented culturally. We find a way to bring them forward into this reality and still not say, "this is totally mine." Because it's not. We have to give integrity to where they came from. There's a way of doing that and that's what I wanted to get at, it's that the vision quest, it's sacred. I don't want to explain it or anything but I want to be able to share that precious experience, that fulfillment of renewing of the world and the beauty of it. That's the way it goes in the song. That's the way of our people.. Song is really one way of expressing the inexpressible.

Lee Maracle: One of the difficulties with English for us is that the analysis is largely on the surface and our sensibility is in the communicacy. And in a great deal of your poetry is coming from within and from a very long ways past and it's going a very long ways into the future in one moment, and language should serve that. Then it's an imagined self, it's a concrete self, it's a past self, it's a future self and it's all embraced in that one moment that these words fall and that breath is exchanged and that thought is embraced and shared. All of those things happen at once. So saying it's identity work or saying it's a style or this or that, doesn't serve. I want to get to that point that when Scott Momaday is looking at things from all the angles, it is like that. The only way that I can imagine it is that it's a round dance of perception. It's constantly moving, so that's why it's so hard to nail down. At the same time it's so beautiful to imagine. I think of that poem at the beginning of <u>Slash</u> and it's these little words that are written forever: "She remembers talking and playing with words in long chains." I remember reading those words, it took me back to before history began. It seemed to take me to the bottom of the sea, far into the future.

Greg Young-Ing: This discussion has brought to mind a quote that I use in my paper when I try to describe some of the unique characteristics of Aboriginal literature. It's a quote from Kimberly Blaeser. Before she made this statement she was talking about the linear and chronological nature of European literature and she points out characteristics unique to Aboriginal literature. She says, "In contrast it gives authority to all voices involved in the story instead of a monological voice speaking out as if it also had ultimate authority. It gives authority into the voices of animals and messages given by spirits and natural phenomenon. It stretches across large spaces of time, ranging in from ancient times to the present to the future displaying the native concept that all time is connected and actions can transcend time." So that's what Kimberly Blaeser wrote. What we were discussing just made me think of that quote.

Kateri Akiwenzie-Damm: I was thinking of memory and how we experience it. For example, having a memory of something that hasn't even happened yet. I was thinking of what our concept of memory is. Also of things like memories of dreams and other things that, for us, are all a part of that concept but that others might not understand in the same way. Also the remembering of a memory becomes a part of your present reality. It's both past and present simultaneously. That experience of memory also influences the future. The whole concept of time transforms and in the process so do we. We transcend time. What transcends time is external. What is external is spirit. So what seems like simply a definition or defining concept is deeper. It reflects who we are, how we view life, our spirituality. It's really fascinating for me because I think that often we use terms in a way that we understand amongst ourselves but really people outside wouldn't understand it in the same way.

Sandra Laronde: A good friend of mine, who is a white women lawyer, started seeing this man who has an incredible usage of language. "Oh, he's so articulate," she said. I was talking to him, or rather he was talking to me for about a half an hour. It was so boring. Then I realized that my definition of articulate is different. When he was speaking it was one word after the other. There was no rhythm change or dynamic to his speech. I saw no pictures when he spoke. I saw no colour, no imagery. They were words that just kind of hung there. So the definition of what makes someone articulate informs what Kateri was just talking about.

Greg Young-Ing: This forum is really the first opportunity for Aboriginal authors to talk about creative non-fiction, and I'm really glad to have been a part of it.

Maria Campbell: This is really inspiring.

Jeannette Armstrong: One of things that's really exciting to me about this forum is that we are collectively working at a way to share with each other and collectively finding approaches that we can use to look at in depth at each other's work. I would really like this process to continue. This is the first stage of this process. I just want to thank everyone for that.

Drew Hayden Taylor: I'm really honoured to be sitting at this table with such presences. Being part of the process and making it collaborative rather than a solitary thing was something quite delightful and I thank you.

Sandra Laronde: What's really inspiring is to hear about creative process. There's something about how we are all talking here that makes it feel universal. I feel very grateful and very privileged to be here.

Kateri Akiwenzie-Damm: Thanks very much for inviting me here to be one of the peers, to be part of the circle. It's a great honour. *Chi megwetch*. It's so nice to be sitting here talking about breath and memory because that's been part of my thinking and my work for awhile. It just feels so affirming that other people are thinking about these kinds of things and doing this kind of work. It's a reminder that it's not done in isolation even sitting in a room with paper and pencil or a computer. We are never in isolation.

Lee Maracle: Something always dismembers us so we always have to remember ourselves forever. So we're doing something that's forever and I think that's what spirit is to me too. I am so glad to be here. It's obviously medicine that we're making here. I'm so glad you're all sitting here at the same table. It's good.

Maria Campbell: I just want to thank Creator for a good day. I feel privileged to be here.

Rasunah Marsden (Moderator): I'd like to close this session, and I thank you all for coming.

(Closing Prayer)

PART II

JEANNETTE ARMSTRONG

KYOTI AND THE FLESH EATING MONSTERS

It was when Kyoti awoke again after a long, long sleep and was dreaming. Having a nightmare really. Kyoti called the people together. That was at the village up there near the base of the mountains. You remember that big old tree that stands there taller than the others. Well it's the one where everybody met that first time, when everybody got their names. Each of us was there. You remember it was such a great day, when all of us was called and each of us was named and we were each told the work we were to do. Everybody was glad there was finally laws for everybody, because there was chaos before. Nobody could be sure about anything and who was doing what and lots of bad stuff happened.

Well, as you know, we were told that day that some new people were going to come and we each had to give up something so that room could be made for them because they would be really dumb and pitiful. Somehow we had to include them in our laws. We had to prepare the world for them

You know how that old story goes. Kyoti bragged around about getting named first and being one of the main four chiefs to take care of the laws for everybody to get along. But of course Kyoti slept in after trying to stay up all night to be sure and be first, and ended up getting one of the last names on the list, which was Kyoti. It was a name nobody wanted because all Kyoti seemed to be good for was to fool around.

But the work Kyoti got actually was special because Kyoti was the only one from us who wasn't content to just be. Kyoti always tried to figure out all kinds of ways to outsmart others who were stronger or bigger or faster in order to prove that

Kyoti should have had that name. And so Kyoti did lots of stupid things. Kyoti always found out what not to do and so in that way was pretty good for showing those new people what they shouldn't be doing. So Kyoti was able to make a few laws for the new people that none of us could have thought of, to keep them out of danger until they figured out our main laws. Anyway, Kyoti ended up doing things which seemed impossible to us and Kyoti ended up being the most famous of us all. All the new people learned about Kyoti, even in their different languages.

So that was why Kyoti got sent around to make a few other laws, too, like for the monsters. Kyoti wasn't brave, mind you, it was just that Kyoti was too crazy to know better. Kyoti got to travel around looking for all the monsters. They were the ones, you remember, who sulked and said they weren't going to give up anything for anybody, let alone the stupid new people. They said they would make their own laws and they would make names for themselves, They ate up whatever they came across and were a danger to all people because they were out of place. They weren't part of the laws. They were consumers.

You remember how they made them laws to balance it out so everybody got to live without anybody getting wiped out. Everybody got to have a body for awhile with a name in a place where they lived along with everybody else. Everybody eventually had to give their body back so others could be. Even Kyoti was in agreement. It was strong and worked.

For a long time Kyoti went around and changed things by finding ways to trick those flesh eaters to agree to change so the people-to-be could finally come. Finally almost all of the flash eaters were either changed to come under the laws or were banished. Some were sent into the ground, some into the waters and some way up to the stars where there were no people. Some tiny flesh eaters were banished to the thick trees and big swamps, others were changed into worms and bugs to eat up only dead flesh. There were the big monsters who tried to run away but starved and froze as the world changed. Some of the meanest ones agreed to leave people alone only if people left them alone. They became invisible.

Well the story is pretty long, if you remember, the main thing is that the new people could live because the flesh eaters were under control so there would be not such total chaos. Mind you living would always be hard but if the laws were kept, things would go okay, and only when the laws got broke and somebody got too greedy then the flesh eaters would come out and sure enough somebody would get wiped out. Then everybody would tow the line again for a long time after.

The thing that's strange in the new world is that the new people are really weak. They don't seem to have any real place in the world, like us. They didn't seem to have real jobs like us. They live off everybody else and they didn't give anything much back to the others. That's a real big problem if they can't somehow learn the laws. So that was why Kyoti got to stick around in this new world for awhile to tell them some of the main laws before going back for a holiday. The rest of it they had to learn the hard way by making all the same mistakes as Kyoti.

Anyway, going back to the start of this story, Kyoti rested for quite awhile but awoke from some bad dreams about the flesh eaters all starting to come back. Lots of them, because the main laws were being broken. Things were beginning to get huge imbalanced, so much so, that many of the banished ones were back. Even a few of the invisible ones, the meanest of the flesh eaters, had become visible again. They were being bothered and ordered around by the new people. And they were mad and were changing and starting to eat living flesh again. Some of the new people were so selfish and dumb they were making it dangerous even for those who listened to Kyoti and who worked with the others to keep the balance.

So Kyoti called the people together to tell them about the consumer nightmares. Kyoti told them about stuff that didn't make sense to any of them. *Kyoti repeated only what the loudest voices shouted*:

SUPERBUGS: WHO WARNS OF GLOBAL CRISIS
According to the World Health Organization, at least thrity new diseases have emerged in the last twenty years and threaten hundreds of millions of people. For

many of these diseases, there is no treatment, cure or vaccine. New virus forms include, HIV/AIDS, Ebola Hemorrhagic Fever, Bovine Spongiform Encephalopathy (mad cow disease), Rotavirus, Hantaan Virus, HTLV-1 and 2 virus, Hepatitis E virus, Hepatitis C virus, Guanarito virus, Sabia virus. New bacteria include, Legionella pneumophila, Campylobacer jejuni, Escherichia coli O157:h7, Helicobacter pylori, as well as new parasites including, Vibrio cholerae O139, and Cryptospridium parvum. In the race for supremacy, microbes are sprinting ahead. Their ability to mutate into drug-resistant strains and man's ability to counter them is widening. Fears are growing over a possible food-chain link, as drug resistant bacteria and other microbes are passed through the food chain, as antibiotics and antimicrobial agents are used worldwide for the production of animal meat.

CANADIAN DOING TRANSGENIC HUMAN-PIG TESTS IN CHINA
SCIENTIST MOVES TESTS ON HUMANS TO CHINA

Instead of waiting Health Canada's permission to transplant insulin-producing cells from pigs into humans, a top Canadian scientist has gained approval from China to conduct the controversial experiment there. The scientific team successfully transplanted insulin-producing pancreatic islets, or cell clusters, from pigs into diabetic monkeys, ending their symptoms. The next step is to test that procedure in humans; Ottawa's approval could take months, even years but things move a lot faster in China. Transplants from one species to another are highly controversial because of the risk of inadvertently passing animal diseases to humans.

MEANWHILE BACK ON THE PHARM

Pharming is a new word in the English language. Pharming, the manufacture of medical products from genetically modified plants or animals, is a quickly growing industry. Pharming's most recent products include goat's milk with a human antibody and sunburn prevention from a genetically modified tobacco plant, now on the market. Pharming's newest products are foods for immunity. The banana, according to reports, is being changed into a vaccine delivery system as is a potato vaccine, now moving to the human testing stage. A recent study estimates animal pharming to be "five to ten times more economical on a continuing basis and two to three times cheaper in start up costs than cell culture production methods." This will set off competition in the industrialized world, and set the stage for pharming crops in poor regions of the world. The future will see large scale tobacco and banana plantations and ranches of genetically modified animals.

CONGRESSMAN AND ENVIRONMENTALISTS UNITE TO STOP INTELLECTUAL PROPERTY RIGHTS ACCORD WITH U.S.
Outraged by recent applications in the U.S. for patents on both widely available medicines and sacred plants, many Ecuadorians have staunchly opposed the U.S. deal. The treaty covers intellectual property rights, and most importantly the patenting of plants and "essentially non biological processes" such as plants cultured in the laboratory and human genetics sequences. Other contentious issues include Micro organisms and microbiological processes can also be patented.

IS YOUR BREAKFAST GENETICALLY ENGINEERED?
Many common foods now use biotechnology in their production and processing. Genetically enhanced corn has increased from 400,000 acres in 1996 to three million acres in 1997 to an estimated 17 million acres planted in 1998. Corn produced through biotechnology is being used in breakfast cereals, taco shells and corn syrup, which is used as a sweetener in soft drinks, baked goods and candies. Soybeans are used in hundreds of food products, including cooking oil, candies and margarine. In 1997, about 20 million acres of the soybeans planted in the United States were genetically enhanced. Milk uses biotechnology because about one-third of all dairy cattle in the United States are given bovine somatotropin, a hormone created through biotechnology, to increase milk production per cow. Genetically engineered enzymes in milk is used in two-thirds to three-quarters of the cheese produced.

TIME TO REGULATE TRADE IN HUMAN TISSUES!
There is now a large and growing South-to-North and North-to-North movement of human tissue, catering to an annual $428 million market which could grow into

a $80-billion-a-year trade in human tissue culture products. This trade is taking place in a policy and regulatory vacuum. The tissue trade is the foundation of a burgeoning industry that depends on patenting and selling pieces of the human body and gathering and providing access to proprietary genomic information. Tissue culture, which is the reproduction of micro-organism, plant, and animal cells in the laboratory, is crucial for the biotechnology industry. When kept under proper conditions, 'immortalised' human cells lines can reproduce in perpetuity and provide an infinite quantity of cells that contain the unique DNA of the original tissue donor.

ACTION ALERT ACTION ALERT ACTION ALERT
FROM THE COUNCIL FOR RESPONSIBLE GENETICS
** Say No To Designer Children!!**
A Federal Government Advisory Committee will consider proposals from a scientist who wants to insert new genes into a fetus. Scientists refer to this process as germ line manipulation because it involves genetic engineering of the human germ cells—eggs and sperm—which carry genetic material passed on to future generations. This is it. This is how it begins. Of all the issues arising from genetic engineering, the threat of germ line manipulation is perhaps the most ominous. The Council for Responsible Genetics (CRG) strongly opposes any attempt to change future generations through genetic engineering. Germ line modification, while commonly performed on other animals, has never been attempted in humans because the ethical consequences are so severe. Do we want a future in which babies are produced according to genetic recipes? (Feel free to borrow wording from this action alert.)

COLLECTING HUMAN SAMPLES IN MONTANA
One of many similar projects to study molecular population genetics of Indigenous people. The essential feature of this project is a collaboration with tribal officials and health care workers, Native American tribal colleges, with research involvement for Native American undergraduates at Montana universities and tribal colleges. Blood samples will be obtained from full-blood members of

Montana tribes, including Assiniboine, Blackfeet, Crow, Northern Cheyenne and Salish-Kootenai.

ONCOMOUSE: THE MOUSE WITH A FULL SIZE HUMAN EAR
Harvard's "Oncomouse" is a genetically engineered mouse. While Harvard has succeeded in getting its patent issued in the United States, Japan and Europe, for the time being, it is unsuccessful in Canada, where you can't patent life forms such as plants and animals. Giving a growing agrobiotechnology market in Canada, many would like to see Harvard succeed.

HAMSTER OVARY CELL LINE MODIFIED WITH HUMAN DNA
A US company uses cell culture to make 'Activase.' A blood-clot-dissolving drug administered to persons who have recently suffered heart attacks. Activase is made by a hamster ovary cell line modified with human DNA that has been spliced into the hamster cells from a human melanoma cell line. Activase takes in $200 million in sales a year. Blood cells from the umbilical cords of newborn infants, which have potential therapeutic applications later in life, are now stored—for a fee—by several companies.

DOLLY: WORLD PATENTS ON SHEEP CLONES INCLUDE HUMANS
CLONING REQUIRES URGENT LEGISLATION
Laws dealing with such practices as human cloning, human-animal hybridization and cell fusion, manipulation of human germ line material, retrieval and use of eggs and sperm from fetuses or cadavers, ectogenesis and the creation of human embryos for research purposes is of utmost importance. These practices are either now possible or under development in agriculture and animal husbandry are rapidly moving into human application. The development and use of these technologies are happening at such a rapid rate that legislation and regulations lag far behind.

Well, back to the story. When Kyoti called everybody together there was a whole lot of the people missing and some new ones that looked pretty weird. The people sat there and listened. Some of them laughed and said, "Kyoti, you're just making that up because nobody could be that stupid. Those newcomers would know by now what happens if those flesh eating buggers are free! Nobody can tell them what to do! They just change and get meaner and eat more living flesh!"

But one of the new ones who was part fish and newcomer said, "But look at me, I'm sitting right here under your nose. I'm part of a bad dream, just like those cows over there with the flesh eaters in their heads."

Kyoti thought for awhile about having to track down and try to find ways to get those flesh eaters to change again. They would just tell Kyoti to go to hell because they only agreed to leave the people alone if the people didn't bother them. Kyoti sat for awhile and looked straight at me and said, "It sure beats me. Maybe one of you guys better straighten them out or kick them outta here before all of us ends up buggered up or wiped out. You remember some of that same bunch got kicked outta that other place for the same thing, earlier on."

Anyway the reason I'm telling you this story is I'm really worried this time. If you don't recognize by now who I am then maybe you need to be sent back to that tree.

DOROTHY CHRISTIAN

WITHOUT SHADES

When I lived in the urban concrete jungle of Toronto, I yearned for my homelands;

I yearned for the smell of sticky pitch as it oozes down the pine trees;

I yearned for the silvery blue sage bushes glinting in the sunlight;

I yearned for the kaleidoscope of blues, purples & greens of Kalamalka Lake, colours like nowhere else in the world;

I yearned for the fields of sunflowers as they reach for the Sun, in absolute adoration;

I yearned for the distinct perfume of the wild rosebushes as they cloister themselves standoffishly, sharing their 'look but don't touch' beauty;

I yearned for the sounds of the cottonwood leaves dancing to the tune of the wind, as he directs their concerto;

I yearned for the multitude of birds serenading each other but I especially missed the call of Blue Jay, laughing at me as if to say, "I know something you don't know!"

I yearned to see the lemon yellow of the first buttercup, as she runs back to tell her Clan, "it's O.K. to come out now"

I yearned for the acres and acres of cherry, apple, peach, and apricot blossoms of the Okanagan Valley;

I yearned for the fat, fluffy cotton batten clouds, changing shapes ever so quickly in the bluest of skies;

I yearned for the pink, orange, and sometimes lavender-blue skies behind the silhouettes of the hills, as the sun left us for the day.

I dreamt of those colours and vibrations as I rode the underground subway trains of Toronto, looking into the vacant eyes of the other walking dead. I walked for what seemed like days on concrete, never touching the green of Mother Earth. Going in and out of tall buildings, following the crowds, like an ant with a purpose. I just wasn't quite sure what the purpose was!

Living in what some people called luxury—totally separate, alone and lonely. Walking in the trendy shops, with blue eyes glaring at me that said, "You don't belong here!" Surrounded by a reality that didn't bring any comfort, yet seeking that comfort in designer clothes, passing shallow friendships, foreign cars and a good-paying job.

Some people called this success.

A false sense of success, in a foreign world of exotic vacations, luxury condominiums, corporate board rooms and asinine cocktail parties. Successful, yet empty of anything meaningful. Successful, according to the society that ripped me away from my Indigenous family as a child and led me to a marriage with a non-Native man. A marriage which took me thousands of miles away from my homelands—to this frightening, empty reality.

As I searched for another reality, I walked away from my marriage, wishing my husband well in that world. I turned away from that foreign world, looking for a reality that spoke to me. A reality where I could see and feel something that reflected the colours, sounds, tastes, and vibrations of the lands I'd left behind.

I wanted a reality with a brown face.

I saw those brown faces everywhere in Toronto. I saw them living on the streets, living in luxurious homes, living in middle class suburbs and struggling in low income housing. Many of them were striving for the same sense of success I had walked away from. Many of them were running. Many of them were seeking. Many of them were lost. Many were there to hit the big time. Many had grown up in the city and never knew the lands of their ancestors. But somehow, we were bound together by our 'Indianness' on the Spadina Rez. Many of us bought hook, line, and sinker, the 'generic Indian' image created by mainstream media. Many of us wore designer clothes with contemporary Indian accessories, dripping in southwest turquoise jewellery. Still engaged in passing shallow friendships, driving sporty cars and working at good-paying jobs. Not all of us, but many of us. Not that there's anything wrong with Indians possessing material things or participating in contemporary activities—what was sad was that most of us didn't realize that all we'd done was put a brown face on our assimilated minds and ways.

After all, what did we know?

Indians were in especially if there was a spiritual, you know a 'mystical woo-woo' quality to it. It was as if the theme song of the Twilight Zone was playing and out of the smoke appeared all kinds of spiritual and cultural teachers in various sizes and shapes. I met guys who claimed to be medicine men and they could sell me the right to do a Vision Quest for only a $1,000. Other so-called medicine men offered me the 'opportunity' to go and live with them to acquire my 'spiritual knowledge.' I saw cultural and spiritual teachers exploiting their naive followers to satisfy their own needs, sexual and otherwise. I remember the very first Sweat Lodge I was in, hands groping my sweaty body and deep down inside I knew that wasn't the way it was supposed to be. I met a man who claimed he had been trained since childhood to be a medicine man and he could join our spirits together. Imagine! One man threatened me with Bear Walk. I was too dense or naive to be afraid. Later, people told me I had every reason to be afraid. All of this in the name of spirituality.

A mystical smoke was added to the beads and the feathers, this was a very scary reality.

That's not to say there aren't spiritual people with integrity. There are those who truly believe in helping people and sharing their knowledge. I saw those teachers too. People with honesty who truly lived their spiritual teachings and whose lives reflected their spiritual laws. I'm not saying that any of it, or all of it, was or is wrong. I'm just saying this was my barefaced reality in the urban concrete jungle. A reality which helped me as a spiritual quester to 'sort out' the real people from the charlatans.

Luckily I didn't give up in absolute disgust. Many of us do. Some of us turn to Christianity with great fervour to become 'Born Again Christians' rather than 'Born Again Pagans.' And some of us turn to the faiths of other cultures, or turn to Eckankar, or some other form of New Age spirituality that offers some solace. Or at least some sense of spiritual safety.

Thankfully, my ancestors were travelling with me, even in the concrete jungle. My people sent a runner, a messenger. They hadn't given up on me. My grandmother who gave me strength as a child was still guiding me. I heard her singing with a drum at the Native Canadian Centre. I remember standing there openly sobbing because I never thought I'd ever hear her voice again.

That voice called me home in 1994. And with me travelled all kinds of romantic notions of my own people and my own lands. 'Home' was like something out of a Hollywood movie. I could see the 'frame by frame' action shots, in slow motion of my family members glowing, as I lovingly remembered them.

It's the year 2000, the beginning of a new Millennium.

I've been back in my home territories in the Okanagan Valley for almost seven years now. I live on the Reservation my grandmother is from. My glowing memories and romantic notions of my homelands, my people and my family, have become an eight mm, black and white, home movie. The summer I came home, my eighty-two year old great aunt was raped and murdered by a man I shared a foster home with.

This is my barefaced reality.

The first spring I was home, I fought with one of my younger sisters. To this day we don't speak. I don't know any of her children. The 60s scoop did its job well. We don't know each other. We don't even know if we like each other. We do share our Mother's blood.

This is my barefaced reality.

My one brother doesn't speak to any of us. There's ten of us altogether. Yet, he was able to bring the Indian people of B.C. together to change the laws on how welfare agencies deal with our children. The welfare took him and I away from the others because we were the eldest male and female. As kids we used to laugh a lot. Nowadays, we're strangers.

This is my barefaced reality.

I see generational family feuds, destroyed family structures, residential school survivors and wards of the court returning to the Reservation without any "know how" of what "community is." I see frustrated leaders not knowing how to put together a healthy family or community, much less a unified Nation.

This is my barefaced reality.

I see power being used to exploit the weaker ones and destroying some. I see men and women in leadership roles covering up for each other in their own "conspiracy of silence" just so they can stay in those positions.

This is my barefaced reality.

I see the welfare dependent mentality thriving and people lashing out at anyone who threatens their meagre handout. I cry as I drive away knowing our own politicians use the fear of the people to meet their own ends.

This is my barefaced reality.

I see Indian people scamming other Indian people, just to survive. Knowing the intellectual theory that the "oppressed are now oppressing their own" doesn't take away the ugly taste in my mouth.

This is my barefaced reality.

I STILL see the ugliness of alcoholism controlling people's lives. And now the grotesque head of cocaine addiction has reared its ugly head. I've even heard that heroin, the Grand Dame of all drugs is making her way into town. Our own people deal drugs to our own kids. We are now killing our own.

This is my barefaced reality.

I came home with such an enthusiasm for healing among my family and community but I didn't realize how deep and how ugly the tentacles of colonization are. They paralyse me. There are times when I feel as if those tentacles choke the life out of me, at every turn.

This is my barefaced reality.

[July, 2000] Recently I had a dream. I'm walking along this path and this big huge rock covers my path and my view on all sides. It's all I can see. It's so big and so black. It's all encompassing. The blackness of it is so dark and in some parts it's shiny and in other parts it fades into slate grey. I'm overwhelmed by the size of it. I step back to see if I can go around it and this voice behind me and to my left says, "Look can you see the faces in the rock? Can you see the pathway?" I squint and I finally see the pathway. It's winding uphill, towards the top. I step back. I see these beautifully carved faces in different parts of this huge black rock mound. I have to look long and hard to see the beautiful faces but once I see them, I'm in awe of their beauty.

I'm climbing the big, beautiful black rock. I'm on the path. I encounter many beautiful faces along the way. ***Reality, without illusion***!

I'm inspired when I see Chiefs in our communities working with traditional values in a very money oriented world. And other Chiefs purposefully bringing back the language to community meetings. ***Reality, without illusion***.

I gain strength from activists who don't give up, even when totally surrounded by the ugly tentacles of colonization. ***Reality, without illusion.***

I see artists being guided to bring forward teachings through some very contemporary ways. ***Reality, without illusion***.

I see people awakening to who they really are. ***Reality, without illusion.***

I see teenagers speaking with the wisdom of old old people. Struggling with what's all around them, fighting for some sanity in an insane world. Reality, without illusion.

I see, hear, feel and touch beauty all around me.

I see a friend's four year old daughter at the IGA saying, "Auntie where have you been? I haven't seen you for a long time." I hear my sister's voice on her answering machine, with this month's inspirational message. I see my brother's email messages as we try to keep connected. I hear my other brother's gruff voice telling me he is going to be a father and I'm the first to know. I hear my uncle's voice telling me what a "good girl" I was when I was little. I see the twinkle in my great uncle's eyes when I bring him my first efforts at canning deer meat. I see the protective look in my nieces eyes as she shows me her son and tells me softly that now I'm a great aunt! I hear my nephew saying, "Thank you Auntie Bophie for bringing me this ribbon shirt." I hear my grown up daughter calling me "Mommy" with a childish little girl voice. I hear the giggles of my other sister as we develop the characters for a script she's writing. I see the beautiful smile of my youngest sister as she tells me she's a gramma. My heart grows big as I witness my sister-in-law's gentle leadership in getting the Sweat Lodge built. I see the sweat pouring down the brow of my youngest brother as he pit cooks salmon for me on the hottest day of the summer—just because he knows I need them for my Feast and Giveaway. I smile as I see the little guy who I knew about first... he's two years old now and a real going' concern. I hear the laughter of the women as we share stories while we prepare for ceremonies. I hear the crackling of the fire as it works with the stones, getting ready for our Sweat Lodge. I inhale the distinct smoke as it penetrates my every pore and curls slowly around every strand of hair as I watch my cousin expertly turn the deer meet on the grates. I see the Elder woman's face light up as she sees me coming around the corner and she tells me, "I've been getting lonesome for you," as she gives me a big bear hug.

My reality, without illusion, is a real life documentary, without any special effects, no slow motion, and no fast forwarding! The characters are real people with all their hurts and pains. Some of them are my family members, each in their healing process. I honour their courage as they walk towards wholeness. The places, the sounds, the tastes and the smells may not be quite as they were when I was a child but they're still here.

I embrace the lands that hold the blood and bones of my ancestors! I tingle all over as the hairs on the back of my head stand on end. I touch the very depths of me as I discover the threads of my ancestry, the bloodlines of my people that weave in and out of the communities of British Columbia. I've found what anchors me to this land.

Last month, I was in Squamish territory to meet with some of the runners of the Peace & Dignity Journeys. The theme for this year's Run is 'FAMILY.' I heard the Elder speak about why they chose that theme. He said, "Without our families we are nobody. Without our families, we wouldn't have our Clans, without our Clans, we wouldn't have our Tribes and without our Tribes, we wouldn't have our Nations. If we don't know who we are, or who our family is, then we may as well be white people!"

I put an Eagle Feather on the main staff of the Peace & Dignity Journeys and asked them to pray for me, for my family, for my community and for my Nation... for all the Nations.

Sylvia Coleman

Population: Delusion or Reality?

In "Population: Delusion and Reality", Amartya Sen acknowledges that there are polar views of the so-called "population problem". One is apocalyptic, predicting complete annihilation of the planet because of locust-like consumption by the masses of people.The polar twin of this apocalyptic view is a complacent view, where the population problem is dismissed on the assumption that population and the environment are self-regulating entities. Sen prefers the latter with some active modifications; but it is the apocalyptic or alarmist view that tends to predominate in the popular and academic mind alike.

As is the case with polar issues, the apocalyptic and complacent views are related and have shared similarities. However, while a few solutions to curb the world's population boom of the past two centuries have been proposed, there appears to be less interest in, or knowledge of, the causes of this boom. The conflict in conclusions originating from sources on population issues begs the question of how the "population problem" can be solved if the conditions that allow population to become a problem are not fully understood. Without first understanding the fundamental causes of overpopulation, we may not be able to answer how to solve it satisfactorily in the future. It might also just be that the fundamental causes of overpopulation are too complex and interrelated to break down into their component parts. But whatever the case, more thought needs to be directed towards this issue of solution, since "superficial" and short-term remedies become ineffective as soon as minor conditions change. Rationally speaking, humans should limit themselves to the carrying capacity of their environment; but given the precedent of the past few centuries, it appears that precisely the opposite has happened. What is it about the "human animal" that has allowed population explosions?

In the eighteenth century, Malthus predicted apocalypse as population outstripped food supply, while Condorcet was a proponent of the Enlightenment view of humans as rational self-regulating beings. Sen continues along the line of the two polarities of the population issue, indicating that solutions to population control align themselves with either "override" methods, or "collaborative" methods of population control. Override methods are those that are increasingly popular in theory today, where interference by a government or other external agency prohibits choice in family planning; this is exemplified by China, where a one-child policy is enforced with fines and incentives. Sen believes that the best way to reduce population is through collaborative policies, where open dialogue, choice and decision-making is encouraged. These collaborative policies focus on female education, reduction of infant mortality, greater economic security, and more participation of women in political arenas and job markets. Sen favours this kind of collaborative policy by comparing the outcomes of collaborative action in Kerala, India, and override action in China; Kerala has a fertility rate of 1.8, which parallels the lowest rates of France, Canada or Sweden. Kerala, while "economically backward", displays impressive social development, dating from policies concerning women's rights and education, put in place by a young ruling queen in 1817. China similarly has a rate of 2.0, but has increasingly serious social problems, including female infanticide and a growing male population, due to the interaction of the pre-existing value put on males, and the one-child rule. It is not in fact clear either whether it is the one-child rule that is the cause of reduced fertility and population, or the coexisting social and economic programs for women.

Sen, like many involved in population policy, focusses on the women who bear the children. Women who are given economic and educational opportunities are far more likely to expand their roles and identities into jobs and schools, and out of the sole role of motherhood. While this incorrectly and problematically implies that women are solely responsible for population issues, it is in many cases a simple and practical focus. Yet Sen seems to miss a salient point: that the imposition of the Northern ideal of lowered or zero population growth cannot necessarily be called a "collaborative" solution to population "excess", regardless of the methods engaged in by (possibly foreign) family planners. In many developing countries, children provide new hands and heads for increased economic opportunity for the family. Children may also represent the major means of increasing a woman's status in her community, contribute to the care of the elderly, and subsequently give the elderly a role, in child care. Western values do not tend to include such roles.

That there is a population problem is actually debated: Germaine Greer argues that overpopulation is essentially a myth generated by people in the richer Northern hemisphere, who are afraid of being "overrun", and that whether we think the world is overpopulated depends on our point of view, concerning what kind of people and what kind of lifestyle should "rule". While Greer appears to at times romanticize Indian slums, and she never mentions, for example, the reality of the suffering caused by disease (which is often related to a lack of hygiene and overpopulation), her portrayal of the "overpopulation myth" is truly food for thought.

Yet, it is hard not to be staggered by the statistics which state, for example, that world population at Malthus' time at the end of the 18th century was about 923 million, and it has taken us a mere two hundred years since then to instate six billion human beings on the planet. Both Sen and Greer point out that the population explosion of the developing countries over the past few centuries is actually similar to, if not less than the population increase of Europe (by percentage) when it was industrialising. Perhaps a larger population in developing countries make do with so much less than Europeans did; it is clear to these two authors in any case that, contra Malthus, the human population has not outstripped the global food supply—a supply which is no longer local, given global markets and famine relief efforts, and driven by high technology—despite the massive increases of people. Sen in fact notes that food prices have been dropping consistently, and that population growth has already begun to slow down, over the past few decades. Developing countries also have been doing their industrialising, in many cases, with the technological discards of the North. That includes birth control methods which Northerners have either given up, like the high-dose oestrogen pill, and sterilisation, which we don't choose on a mass scale, as is often expected in places like India. We sell DDT to the Third World (for mosquito control and garden use) and CFC-based equipment, despite the fact that most of us have banned the former and are phasing out the latter. The IMF supplies Indonesia with billions of dollars of aid, but only under certain conditions, which might not favour Indonesian development. There are speculations about how the North keeps the South in line in order to take advantage of the cheap labour that supports our economies. Whose aims are being promoted here? Is there actually more to this than just X-File-ish, conspiracy theory paranoia?

On an apparently more 'rational' note, Virginia Abernethy is of the opinion that any kind of social development must happen locally, in response to local signals. She states that "development programs entailing large transfers of technology and funds to the Third World have been especially pernicious. This kind of aid is inappropriate because it sends the signal that wealth and opportunity can grow without effort and without limit." (p.88) She does however advocate appropriate aid, like micro-loans, and family planning, "not because contraception is a solution in and of itself, but because modern contraception is a humane way of achieving a small family size [when that is desired]" (p.91). But in the face of political correctness and moral sensitivities, what does one make of the idea that by entering into development work, Northerners are only supplementing the helplessness, and curbing the creativity of other societies to limit their own growth? Further, are we creating some kind of "welfare" mentality among developing nations? Wouldn't this conclusion be somewhat contrary to the solution that Sen proposes, which is that economic and social development as instigated by the North is the way to stem overpopulation? These are all questions that should be answered and not skittered around within the limiting framework of political correctness, which inhibits real debate. But in the end it is not at all clear that these questions can be answered satisfactorily. The population problem is truly complex.

On a final note, it is curious that it is only over the past two hundred years that the escalation of population now requires family planning and development aid. Why all of a sudden have these populations exploded? It is certainly not the case, as has been expressed by at least one person I have met, that "those people have nothing better to do with their time than to make babies".

It is a fact that botanical and barrier contraceptives have been known and used widely since antiquity, by traditional tribes, Europeans, ancient Greeks, and others around the world. Examples of stable populations over recorded time up until the 17th or 18th century AD are reported anywhere one could look. This is not just due to luck: populations can only remain stable in undisturbed societies and do result from fairly simple family planning. But what happened two hundred years ago to negate the millennia of cultural understandings of family planning?

Industrialization without urbanization would be a likely cause. Both Greer and Abernethy point to the culprit of colonialism in general in their writing, and this does fit the dates; rapid industrialization quickly followed colonisation of a country, although it did not immediately lead to the development of large urban centres. While it is difficult to assess exactly how much of an impact colonisation has really had on the populations of developing countries, there can be no doubt that new trade, plantation work, economic opportunities, conversions of religious beliefs and family planning customs, helplessness, pessimism, alienation from families, imported health aid and so on, has completely changed the face of the globe, over the past two to four centuries. But if colonisation is a strong causal factor of today's overpopulation, then it seems that we are now literally dealing with the fruits of our actions; and that the logic which points to 'development' as a way to decrease population could also be the main force behind its very increase.

BETH CUTHAND

FEAST FOR THE FOUR WINDS

The summer sky was heavy with thunder rumbling clear across to the horizon. It was always thundering that summer. I was preoccupied with thunder. My mind crackled with the thunder. A vision of a shield repeatedly invaded my waking thoughts and nightly dreams: a field of deep green grass and a heavy thunder sky, a single bolt of lightening and a black bear walking from west to east. I drew it. I painted it. I sketched it in pastels. Sometimes I created a large shield, sometimes small shields. I was no good at drawing the bear. It seemed like the thunder would never stop.

What did it all mean? I asked my dad about thunder birds. I read everything I could. I read about dragons who bore such a resemblance to the thunder beings. I drew. I read. I wondered. I talked to the Saulteaux. We were always allies. I learned to put out tobacco when the thunderers came. I looked forward to their visits. I would talk to them at night as they rumbled and cracked over our house.

The sky was huge when the thunderers came. They opened a doorway to a reality both familiar and strange—almost indescribable. I saw huge kite ships sailing between the stars. I saw large dark shapes swooping and diving in the nightly storms.

One day I arrived at work to learn that a Taoist Monk was visiting and would do some 'work' with us. Why this didn't surprise me was probably because I was already in the midst of such intense spiritual experiences that the appearance of one small Taoist Monk at my workplace seemed ordinary. The Monk introduced us to Tai-Chi, told us to stop locking our knees. Breathe in. Breathe out. Laugh sometimes. We sat with him in a tea ceremony. The aesthetics of the green frothing tea splashing in a cup was like the sounds of butterflies bathing, small tinkling bells and dragons. That night, I was not surprised to meet in my dreams a wonderful gray and purple dragon who told a few knock knock jokes and invited me to take a ride with him. He flew me past the moon, Mars, Jupiter, Pluto; out around the cosmos and back home all the while trailing a pulsating silver cord which anchored us firmly to earth. The sheer fun of it sustained me for many years. What a trip.

As a result of the grey dragon, I knew that dragons and thunder beings were one and the same: beings who balanced the earth and the sky. It sounds absurdly simple placed in a sentence on the page, but at the time the wonder of it was almost overwhelming. There were times when I wondered if I might be blown off the earth by the power of the thunderers. The top of my head felt like it would break open at any minute. I dreamed and wondered where it was all leading. Then my friend Phyllis disappeared.

*   *   *   *

I didn't see her for three weeks. When she returned, she called, "I've been on a trip. I nearly died but I'm all right now. I'm at the hospital. I want to see you but I want to warn you that I've lost a weight. I don't want to shock you."

I went up to the hospital. Her husband Joe was sitting on a chair outside her door. "She's waiting for you," he said. "She's been very sick but she's going to live." I entered the room and walked to her bedside. Her eyes never left mine. "Don't tell the others," she said. "They're not ready to know yet." I promised I wouldn't tell them what I saw in her eyes. She was dying.

Strangely, it was not a shock. Somehow the dragon and the thunder made anything possible—even inevitable. Like the thunderers transforming the energy of earth and sky, a transformation had come powerfully upon my friend in a very short time. Where three weeks ago she had been in shining good health, now she was near death. It too was inevitable.

I went home and sat outside alone drinking coffee and smoking cigarettes one after another. The mosquitoes damn near ate me alive. My children hovered nearby wondering why mom had retreated so far into herself. I did not get sentimental reviewing our friendship or her short life. She wouldn't want me to waste an evening on things so small and insignificant in the face of what was waiting for her. She knew there was an ineffable force that would enfold her and bring her peace. I prayed that her death would come soon and that she wouldn't suffer.

That night I dreamed of the Feast for the Four Winds.

* * * *

I was sitting in a large teepee holding a Pipe. An old man sat beside me holding a Pipe also. We sat facing south with concentric circles of people surrounding us, people from every corner of North America, Asia, Africa, Europe... old people, children, women, men. Everyone appeared happy and relaxed. The old man told me to tell the people what to expect during the ceremony and I began to speak like this,

"My relatives. We are here today to honour the Four Winds. Who ever hears the winds can attest to their words. They know that we are small and weak in the force of the greatness of creation. They know we are nothing without the land. They see that we come from every direction and that we are small and vulnerable before them."

"Today we have gathered to honour them with a feast. Many generations have told us that the winds bring to us and they also take away. Sometimes it is not clear if they are taking or bringing. The winds are common to us all."

"Because we are gathered here in North America, we will eat the foods from the Four Directions of this land: Salmon from the western doorway, caribou from the north, squash from the east, corn from the south, and wild rice from the heart of the land."

At this the people nodded and murmured together. The old man held up his Pipe and began to pray and I held my Pipe likewise and a prayer rose up in me.

"Great mystery
you who are neither male nor female,
not bound by language or custom,
We are so small
in your presence.
Pity us.
Help us to respect and honour each other
and accept our humanity."

* * * *

That was all. As dreams go, this one went unfinished. But I woke up the next day excited to tell my friend about my wonderful dream. I was sure the dream belonged to her. She looked at me and smiled. Her gums had started to bleed and she was even thinner than when I had last seen her. "It's too soon" she said. "People are not ready for that feast." And she closed her eyes. I felt a wretched disappointment. If we just got everybody together we could pull it off. We could have such a feast that day in the hospital.

Phyllis touched my hand and I held it gently so as not to break it. I could feel my cheeks getting wet. She squeezed my hand. "Someday but not now. Go on, you go now. Have some fun. See a movie."

That was the last time I saw her alive. She died that night.

For eighteen years I carried the Feast for the Four Winds in my heart waiting for the right time, the right place, the right people to materialize so the feast could happen in real life. Sometimes I would pause and worry that perhaps the conditions would never be right until I realized the spirits were laughing at my foolishness. What is time to spirits anyway? What is place? Who are the right people?

This is the feast. In these words, I celebrate survival, love, redemption, peace:

She brings the dreams
for Joe

She weaves the sky,
body
and
feathered breath
caressing
the heart of all that is.

She brings the dreams
that keep the buffalo
returning
to the sea of grass
season to season,
birth to death
to birth to death.

She sings the songs that
spin the world
that bring the winds
to stir the dust
of blue horses
humming.

Clouds whisper stories
of her sweet rain and
antelope
prance in prairied light.

Stones speak slowly
to little people who
have known
her for millennia.

This is the secret
they whisper.

These are her words:
There is no magic here
but what is natural
Dreams are the seeds of reality
choices for our making

I am the Voice
for every one who takes it back

I am the voice of waves crashing on stone shores.
I am the voice of raindrops on glass refracting rainbows.

I am the voice of fiercesome bear woman doing battle
for lost souls seeking light.

I am the voice of mother cooing love songs to sweet babes.

I am the voice of woman calling wolves, cracking ice shields
covering broken hearts.

I am the voice of night whispers, moans and soft sounds
of skin on skin, bones reverberating wild delight.

I am the voice of thunder rumbling deep fire over
earth,
my tears bring light.

* * * *

In the late summer of 1989, I sat with my brother and sister-in-law in their
Sweatlodge where we prayed for the good health and happiness of our family. I
had known, as mothers know, that something was not right with my children and
hadn't been for some time. I was worried for their future, hoping that somehow I
could find the key to unlock the mystery of their unhappiness. As we prayed
together, I felt myself moving into the dream place of visions. Darkness swirled
around me and then I saw my sons in the bedroom of our Vancouver home. They
cowered in the corner of their lower bunk crying and begging a hovering man not
to harm them. Over and over, my older son cried. "We're too little." The man did
not hear his plea and raped them both all the while warning them softly that if
they told me, I would no longer love them. Their terror was pitiful to watch. I felt
sick. Appalled beyond words, I gasped for breath. I felt leaden and heavy. I cried
"All my relations!" and the Sweatlodge was opened.

The realization that my sons were defiled so deeply was almost beyond
comprehension. I sat rocking in shock. The vision was true. I felt it deep inside. I
wailed and cried and cried and cried. It all became so clear to me. I sat with my
brother until nearly midnight crying and talking, crying and talking.

But a vision is only a vision until reality provides some proof.

Where would I find the help I needed to heal my wounded family? Would my boys
have the courage to face the truth. Because so many Aboriginal people all over the

country were beginning to talk about sexual abuse, I knew enough to know that each person heals in his or her own time. There could be no forcing it with my sons. I confided in dear friend and medicine man who told me forcefully without equivocation that the very best thing that I could do for my sons was to take care of myself first. What was it that I most wanted to do?

Again the warm safety of the Sweatlodge provided me with my answer. At the end of the third round of a particularly hot and difficult sweat, the door was opened and a coyote peeked inside.

She tilted her head at me and I swear she smiled! Then she turned and trotted away heading south. "Hey John!" I gasped to my brother. "Did you see that coyote?" But he just smiled and looked inscrutable. We finished the fourth round and as I crawled out of the lodge, I heard a voice say "University of Arizona-the old stories."

* * * *

That's how I came to be in Tucson in the fall of 1990. I and my twelve year old son Luke moved to the desert so I could work on a Masters in Creative Writing. N. Scott Momaday was there teaching a course in Oral Traditions. Joy Harjo was there to mentor me and reinforce the truth that my words were more than me. I loved the desert. I loved school. I loved the one hundred other writers in the program who showed me I was not alone.

Luke was not so lucky. The landscape confused him. He would tell me that he couldn't figure out the rules at school. The kids were different. I drove him to school every day for two weeks. I had the uneasy feeling that his travelling on the school bus would be problematic. Finally, we both decided the day had come to ride the long yellow school bus.

But that afternoon, when it was time to go home, Luke walked out the wrong door and couldn't find his bus. Deciding that it wasn't too far to walk home, Luke began to walk. It was one hundred and ten degrees that day. He had no water. He had no idea he was walking the wrong way.

At 5:30 I called the police. They chided me for not calling them sooner. I was surprised they would take this disappearance seriously. They were wonderful. I was shocked. Within twenty minutes, two members of a special family unit knocked on my door. After questioning me, they decided Luke was not a runaway. They asked for a picture and detailed description. A search was mounted. Night fell. Helicopter crisscrossed the sky. I was contacted every half hour to see if Luke had made it home.

As time passed, all available cars were called into the search. I became more and more afraid that some perverted sadist had abducted my boy or worse. At 9:30, a policeman phoned to see if Luke had arrived home yet. He informed me they were going to call out the National Guard! This was too weird. No Canadian cops would bother searching for one missing Indian kid until at least 24 hours had passed and even then you'd have to bang your shoe to get some action. Now the National Guard!

Five minutes later, a cop phoned. Luke had been found. He was hungry and thirsty but appeared to be fine. He had gone into a convenience store to get a drink of water and the cashier, knowing that a boy matching his description was missing, had phoned the police.

After that night, Luke was never quite the same. Quietly, the world began to unravel and Luke slid slowly, slowly down the string.

* * * *

The boy huddled beside the prickly pear. His hands were swollen by the hundreds of punctures made by the cactus as he picked the ripe red fruit. His mouth was stained scarlet like a baby sucking a blood filled breast. The boy was silent. He had seen his death and there was nothing more to say. He knew now that time had curved in on itself. He had always known it was possible.

He thought about his mother's blue car and knew he was not of that time. The desert stretched before him untouched by roads, smog, or any thing man made. He wondered who his mother was now and he became lonely—so terribly lonely.

The boy was exhausted. He had never felt so tired. He remembered running and running through the street of the city—a stranger in a stranger land. He had not belonged to that hot desert city. The cactus, the heat, the noise of the helicopters, the dryness did not belong to him. He was terrified as the black jeep came closer and closer, the expression on the dark man's face was intense, like a cat about to pounce on a baby squirrel.

Who would believe him? Who would ever understand the darkness or the fear?

"I will hide from my death," he thought. "I will become a seed until my mother finds me, then I will live again."

Dark Moon
Body memorizes voices caught
in the throats of wolves.
Wind echoes through this
forest of night terror and mind sweat.
The heart hum dies in this
cacophony.

Punched walls and torn flesh
cringe as
harsh words trace
phantoms imprinted
on skin too thin
to take the line.

Sharp lies cut this dark moon soaked in blood.

The red fruit rotted into the sand. Inside the black seed the boy felt the terrors crawl. He made himself very, very small. He remembered the times he had tried to describe the terrors to his mother but he had no words then not even now. The dark forces came nearer and nearer. He ran and he ran-down the concrete path, he ran screaming, the knife raised overhead dripping blood. Somewhere far away he could hear his mother calling him.

* * * *

"Luke! Luke! Don't hurt the babies."

It was September 26, 1991. I remember the sky was pink and the late afternoon light made everything magical. That's what I remember as I ran after Luke. Toddlers played outside in the coolness of the setting sun. Golden light bounced off their innocent little faces as they laughed and gurgled at the strange silly boy who ran through their play area. Luke's face was wild. His eyes stared out of his head as he ran with the big knife. One of his friends ran along beside him calmly talking to him. "Luke, your mother wants you to bring her knife back. She needs it to cook dinner. You'd like to eat dinner wouldn't you? Come on Luke, why don't you let me carry the knife?" But Luke lost him in the desert that bordered the university housing site.

The boy crouched on the gray rock perched high on the hill. The sky shone blood red and through the trees, shadows roared. He cowered under their hands and teeth, smothered under their will. The shadows taunted him. Their voices roared through his mind. "No one is going to love you now. No one is going to love you now." The boy drowned in the noise and the fading light of the blood sun.

I wondered if Luke would ever return. He was gone. Luke was no longer in that shell of a body. His knuckles were cracked and bloody. Other kids on the ward kept away from him. He raged. He pounded the walls and doors, his body, his head. I would search his eyes for a sign, some sign that my boy was there. He would growl, averting his eyes. All I read was shame.

I had been going to the hospital every day, sometimes twice a day if my schedule permitted. Luke began to threaten me. "I could kill you right now," he'd say and I believed those eyes that glittered back at me. My boy was gone and something malevolent had taken his place. Finally, the doctor asked me to stop visiting. The treatment team wanted to see if my absence might shock Luke back to reality. It didn't work. Luke got worse. A few days later, the family councillor called to tell me that Luke was locked in the padded room and put on twenty-four hour watch. This meant that someone would sit in the room with him continually until he broke or until he required medication to put him out.

The next ninety-six hours were interminable to me. I went to class. I did my reading. I couldn't write. I barely ate. I prayed continually. I begged. I bargained. I demanded. I wept. I tried to find my Luke but he had severed the silver cord that bound us mother to son.

Then three days into his sojourn in the padded room, a fellow poet and wise woman phoned me. She was in Tucson to do a reading. "Tomorrow at ten I'll be in my hotel room. I've arranged some time and some help to find Luke. You stay home alone and at ten tomorrow morning I want you to anchor me as I go out in search of him. He needs to be reminded that he chose this life. He has an obligation to live it."

The next morning, I did as she instructed. That afternoon at four o'clock, I got a phone call from the hospital. "Luke is back. He wants to start working at therapy. He'd like to see you." I jumped in my car and drove to the hospital stopping along the way to pick up a helium filled balloon which said "Welcome Back."

"So Luke," I said, after we had settled in his room, "Did you see your friend?"

"Oh yes I saw... (he always called her by her complete name). She told me to get back to work. I chose this life."

Ah, my Luke. He's the bravest human being I have ever met and I am forever grateful that he chose to stick around.

Songlines at Dreamers' Rock
for Luke

You know me by my dress green mallard blue
swaying deep in this cave of bones
Indigo dreamer dance with me

You hear my purple light singing to dawn and dusk
and you know it too:
beginnings and endings are
all one fiercesome love
for the gifts of dreamers and
fools.

I know you by your clear blue songs
and boy's breath
dreaming life in the indigo night.

I hear your star time singing and I know it too:
time and the stars end
where
God lives.

Purple hearted dreamer sing with me
To this ancient earth
these songlines at dreamers' rock. Life is. Life is.

* * * *

The Heroes of the Revolution

for LM, SP, SPD, EB, JS, FPD, LBH, DKG,
JJM, JA, LJ, EC, CO, CS, WS, VM, JC, WG,
JH, GB, MM, MC, SK, LR, BY, EO, JCA, JI

So what's the bottom line
to all this shit?

What lies will survive the fires of
this goddamn war?

Don't speak! Don't feel!
It's all in the past! In the past!

We will speak!
And face the killer of our
liberation SILENCE

We will yell scream
and howl the undead past
cry pain in the bones

miscarried lives and suicides.
Don't speak! Don't speak!

The heroes of the revolution
speak secrets:
the scaled serpent rising
forked tongue sucking
numbed children travelling
to dark worlds

where solitude is safe.
We say what has not been said:

"Aunty beats her boy."
"Uncle raped me when I was four."
Don't speak! Don't Feel!
It's all in the past! In the past!

smothered
in the excrement of silence

the undead hide
behind
walls of mindless television,
video games, compulsive sex
and iron so pumped it sweats.

We do what must be done:
avenge the silenced with our words
live our truth
claim our heroism
celebrate beyond survival

Don't feel! Don't

Heroes of the revolution feel
pain, sorrow, anger, joy
compassion, love, hate, ecstasy

We
dance this life, play the child
try new things, cry and laugh

fall in love.

We take back what has been stolen.
We take back what has been stolen.

Chris T. George

... thoughts on life, death & the fickleness of god...

... it seems that, upon reflecting on my past few years of life, death was never really an option... about four years ago i had made a radical change in my life... i attended an aboriginal youth conference and it was there that my new life began... from that day, up until this very day, my focus has been on life... living a clean, balanced life in which i am a productive role model for myself and children... when i decided to change my life around, my daughter was only a year old and my son was not yet born... it was for her, and later, for both her and my son that i remain focussed on a positive journey in life... i am trying to provide for them an option... an option of sobriety and ceremonial life... an option in contrast to the stereo-typical life of the "rez-kid"... i was taught that the best way to teach a lesson is to live it for yourself... teach by doing... and i say again, that is why i remain focussed on a positive journey in life... the keyword in that aforementioned sentence would be "life"... how could i be a role model for my children if i am dead?... so you see, for death is not an option... yet for the past year or so i have been thrown into thoughts of mortality... in all my years i have never been close to death... no one close to me ever died... i have attended only two wakes in my life and they both left me with an uncomfortable feeling... i am told that death is as natural as birth... our journeys do not begin here on earth, nor do they finish here... death is a doorway... it is something to be welcomed... it is something to be celebrated... those are good teachings and they were told by wise people... yet they have no real meaning for me... i can not put them into any sort of context because of the fact that i have had no closeness to the dying process... so, as good as those teachings are... to me, they are only "theories", with no context... i do not know how i will react when death claims my mother, or my siblings... in one of my classes at university, the professor asked to pretend that we only had three days left to live... what would we do?... at first it was a rather clinical question, void of emotional content... however, when i started thinking of my children and what would happen to them, i became rather scared... scared for my children... i do not think that anybody is secure enough in themselves and secure enough in the way they have raised their children to let them go... even if you have imparted with your children the utmost honourable and peaceful lessons of life... i am not sure if any parent is ready to leave their children alone... alone in this world... maybe it is because i am young and my children are young, that i feel this way... i look to my friend and elder dave christie... to me, he has been a father... he has taught me many valuable lessons that will be with me for as long as i am around... when i look at his situation, i see the epitome of acceptance... he understands his role... his role in life, as a husband, a grandfather, a father and his role in death... he has had years of life experience and it is from that which he draws upon to walk in this world... i listen to his stories and when i do, i realize that i am young... my life experience, however endearing or valuable it has been, it is just beginning... selfishness and envy... are those the underlying factors in our lack of acceptance and our fear of death?... are we afraid to let go?... afraid to miss out on something... are we prepared to die?... what is there left to do?... all of those times that we hesitated in our past, whatever the situation... is it that hesitation that is not allowing our consciousness to leave this world... some altered form of regret for not asking that certain person out for coffee... or not taking that spontaneous trip to a grateful dead concert... when you look at it, the majority of our life is lived in fear... from the time the doctor slaps our ass and we enter this world screaming... there is fear... for a brief moment of about five years we have no understanding of life or death... no fears... yet, our parents, our aunts and uncles perpetuate their latent fear of the dark... of the "boogie-man"... or that certain part of town... they perpetuate those fears onto our pure, un-educated mind... as we mature and grow, those latent fears allow us to hesitate, hence leading to regrets and "should-ofs"... and before you know it you're eighty six and you feel a sting in your left arm, you clutch your chest and fall down, you stop breathing and for the briefest of moments your life flashes before your very eyes... all those missed opportunities... then you exhale for the last time... is the fear gone?... does it leave with that last breath?... who knows?... there are many things in this world that we cannot answer... and there are things that we should not answer... science is not "all-knowing"... neither is theology, philosophy or even the stars... sometimes we need to do, that which is expected of we humans... a friend of mine shared a personal story with me... her father was dying... he was in a hospital and in a very bad way... a few days before he passed, he had a vision... in this vision he was spoken to... the voice introduced himself as god... the voice told him that he would answer one question for him... my friend's father asked simply, "what is it that we are meant to do here on earth?"... the voice replied sort of indirectly, as god does from time to time... "look at the salmon... the salmon knows its role and the salmon does its job and is happy... the salmon will save the world"... a few days later her father died, but his vision has been passed on... i was honoured to hear it... i then asked myself, what is it that a salmon does?... i guess that is up to the individual to interpret... when we enter this world, as we pass through the birth canal and are received for the first time by human hands, we are not yet alive... we have a purplish-blue skin tone and we are not yet breathing... the doctor promptly cleans our mouth and with a pat on our backside we inhale earth's gift for the very first time... it is at that time life enters our body... that gift allows us to cry... to grow... to procreate... that gift allows us to live... and when our journey closes to an end... whether we are struck down at an early age or live to be a hundred and twenty-three... as we feel the presence of night... and as death hastens to the ultimate finale... the last earthly gesture we offer is an exhale... that gift that allowed us to live when we first dared to breath, leaves us... who could define that gift?... does it need a definition?... when i first heard that story, i concentrated my thoughts upon the gift itself... what does that gift mean to me?... i see the gift of air as our spirit... i guess now i am focussing my thoughts on the gifts that come between our first and last breath... i think that it is that period of time in which we will find our acceptance... learn what we must from the salmon... be happy... and learn the lessons of selfishness and envy and let them go... and be able to deal with our fears... if we live our lives to the proverbial "fullest"... if we leave behind hesitation and regret, would we then be prepared to die?... is it a good day to die?... or is it a good day to live?... maybe life and death are the two halves of one whole and the important thing to realize is that sometimes... it is just a good day...

nicole (migizikwe) hetu

IDEOLOGY: THE SEDUCTION OF A MIXED-BLOOD IDENTITY

A beginning...

Ideology, identities, the seduction and the consequences of the constructs we either consciously or unconsciously 'buy into' or succumb to are psychologically damaging to our mental, emotional and spiritual state. Specifically damaging are the affects of these constructs on individuals in a community of First Nations people. Whether these communities that we identify with are urban or not, we are affected by the ideologies, influences and forces of the dominant colonizing society. It is this process that I wish to examine and explain. I will explore through my own personal experience how 'ideology,' as Althuser defines it, draws us into particular constructions of identity.

I intend to work through this exploration of identity constructs using three particular experiences that have particular significance to me, one of which is ongoing. The ongoing situation is my brother's perpetual state of gross chemical consumption: drug addiction. In his reflection, I am also mirrored. Second, I'll look at the experience of defining and determining who is and who isn't an 'indian' using the analogy of the 'Indian scale' as a metaphor. Third, the blood quantum definition and the legal dis-enfranchisement of Indigenous[1] Women will be explored.

---

[1] I prefer to use the internationally recognized term that defines Indigenous peoples as the First Peoples of a land or territory. The Webster's Dictionary defines *indigenous* as, {L} *indigenus*, fr. L. indigena, n., native, fr.OL indu, endo, in within} 1 : Having originated in and being produced, growing, living, or occurring naturally in a particular environment or region 2 : Innate, inborn *sin* see NATIVE.

I will also not capitalize the "i" in "indian" when referring to the colonial usage and legal term used by the dominant government and settler society. I will use capitalized "I" in Indigenous because it is not merely an adjective, but I use the term as a proper pronoun when referring to (Native, Indian, First Nation, Aboriginal) people, I prefer to call us Indigenous Peoples.

I intend to consider the social consequences and contradictions within this 'gender' violation initiated by the colonial government. I, myself am a so-called Bill C-31er, a product of a particular mixed-blood marriage of a Saulteau mother to a 'white' Francophone father.

I wish to begin with a quote by bell hooks who is speaking about theory. She begins with pain. It is this element of my own pain that I wish to begin with. I feel that we grow from experience, especially through that which has moved us: anger, hurt, pain or humour. These elements of emotion are the fuel to the process of theory liberation that happens through reaching out and through the sharing of our lives through our stories. bell hooks shares, "I am grateful to the men and women who dare to create from the location of pain and struggle." (hooks, 1994:74) It is this continuous process of self-critique, thought, and reflection that allows us to formulate words that give voice to our hurt and pain, through our lived experience.

I am writing this reflection paper in my own language. A language accessible to the people with whom I share my own common experience: my family. This paper is a gift to my only 'blood' or biological brother. I am writing it for his life. I am also writing it for my own selfish intentions, in an attempt to offer hope, to unravel the ideologies that impress themselves upon our lives as mixed-blood peoples. These ideologies encompass sociological conditions that we are either excluded from and/or forced to include ourselves within. This is one of the countless attempts to understand the differing ideologies that have worked to produce us and continue to do so. I feel there is an important therapeutic and rewarding act taking place despite the pain of this process or the brutal truths that may torture us. In the end, we will be better, wiser individuals due to this reflection. It is a journey about my brother, that pertains to me. It is a critique and an exercise I have been involved in since my political birth as an Indigenous person twenty-five years ago.

I will explore the psychology and the harm of assimilation and the implications of colonialism. Colonialism and assimilation continue to manifest themselves in the society at large, but specifically for people who are the oppressed in this relationship. Assimilation. It is a process that can grow within itself inside of me: internalized racism. Colonizing is so pervasive that an individual can be affected, changed and harmed by it without another individual actually inflicting this or dictating this harm.

A sharing...

I just returned home. I am drained, heavy with emotion, and once-more angry. I just saw my baby brother. Surprised? I guess it's not a normal experience one has with a sibling, hey? Indeed I did meet with a person, who looks like my brother and answers to his name, but it's not the same person who I should recognise or who I have known for the past twenty-three years. No, I have a much more difficult time conversing with or finding a commonality with this person whom I love, as I love my own life. I see a reflection of my own self and in a righteous manner, I critique, analyse and hypothesize his life and its happenings. At the same time I attempt to try to find understanding, as our lives are intertwined and shared. I too, am affected by my brother's drug addiction. In fact, each time we meet (which is not too often) I search for familiar or relative words that would make him happy. I try to share positive things about my life (without trying to sound judgemental, making him feel inept). However this is all a struggle, trying to find a way to relate and offer love without sounding condescending or patronizing. I'll explain more to shed light on this situation.

My brother is addicted to synthetic heroin commonly recognized as morphine. Morphine is the cleanest, thus purest drug from this opiate. Heroin is a crushed, unclean, derivative of morphine. It is bought and crushed down with other impurities and harmful additives such as aspirin, angel dust (pcp), Tylenol, etc. He (at one time) shot, or injected sixty milligrams, three times daily. A shot of morphine is enough to knock an injured person out, one who has a crushed body frame, or head injury, for twelve hours, and relieve that person from pain. Morphine compensates for the overload of shock that the body is experiencing. The natural opiates produced by the endorphin in your brain can not alleviate the trauma your body is experiencing, so morphine has to compensate for this pain.

My brother takes this average dose for the drug addiction he has been consumed by for the past five years. When he can not acquire morphine from the streets, he will involve himself in any methadone program nearby. He needs the methadone to save his body from the shock it would have to bear because of the lack of the regular intake of morphine to which his body is addicted. His addiction controls him. He seems to have no choice in this cycle. He must feed his physical need for the drug or his body will go into convulsions and withdrawal.

My brother's story is an analogy. It is representative of the internalized hatred our communities live with. The only alternative my brother thinks he has to mask, deny and escape through, is his addiction for the realities he has seen and continues to see. He is perpetuating a cycle that is still rampant in our communities. It is a cycle of apathy, and the overwhelming and heavy feeling of hopelessness. Addiction is an alternative. This asphyxiation is at times difficult to see beyond or above, especially since we have been conditioned to believe we are without control and consumed by addiction. This is affirmed in stereotypes and in the representations we see around us, as 'indian' people.

You might be asking yourself, "How does this tie into ideology?" I think it is very appropriate in the sense that my brother's state of addiction and need to compensate for his hurt and confusion is an example of the destructive cycles that consume and drive us. I believe his is seduced by exploitive and stereotypical images of the 'Indian' (as I am most often living my life of exploitation). We often internalize racism and perpetuate it, colonizing ourselves, however holding ourselves, our families or our culture responsible for our state. In a sense we buy into, or believe what the dominant culture states that we are. One cycle of our addiction is ideological and carried out through the assimilative attempts in the colonizing process. My brother's identity is in a state of confusion, perplexity, and hurt (in my judgement). This constant questioning and uncertainty leaves him asphyxiated, shackled, and bound to the colonialist and stereotypical images that he is surrounded with and to the realities that he/we grew up surrounded by. This socialization due to colonialism and assimilation causes great dysfunctions and imbalances in how we see ourselves! In how we see each other? We confuse our own definition of ourselves as Indigenous people living with constructed "indian" identities those which have their roots in imperial thought and in the imperial intentions of the dominant settler society.

What complicates the situation is that we begin to think that we have our own freewill and that we are determining our own existence, as well as who we are as individuals and as a whole society. In the mere act of choosing what options to be hailed by or that hail us, we are succumbing to what the dominant society is offering us. We are then buying into the belief or identity that we are hailed by. We are consequently, whether willingly conscious or not, participants or perpetrators of that society.

With our histories and contemporary education, thought, language and cosmology being controlled by the dominant Euro-Canadian forces... "how can we imagine a new language when the language of the enemy keeps our dismembered tongues tied to their belts?" (Alexie, 1994: 152) It is difficult to explain with a tangible articulation, a reality or world view or space that is entirely our own Indigenous discourse and paradigm. A world-view free of colonial impressions free of assimilation. I am not saying that our world does not exist, because there is a discourse, a counter-narrative, and reality that belongs to Indigenous people. However, I will state that there are few communities to my knowledge that do not have colonial influences or government forces attempting to establish control, both within the community and outside of this community.

Are you 'Indian' or are you 'white'?

Considering this question leads us to Modernist Western Binary/Positional Thinking. According to the western cosmology, the 'Indian' identity is constructed in difference. It is what a Western European is not, or, if similar, it is the same according to the dominant, judging, comparing and analysing society. The 'Indian' identity is always according to the dominant ideology and thus constructed. Binary/oppositional thinking is upheld by our differences according to the colonizing culture, for example: capitalism vs. egalitarianism, patrilineal vs.

matrilineal, textual vs. oral.

There exists in 'Indian country' a discourse of defining and determining who is and isn't 'indian.' Some of these judgements are rooted in the blood-quantum definition and policies administered by DIAND and the Indian Act. These original policies were carried out by indian agents in the 'treaty making' process and still continues in Band politics and thus affecting the mind-set. The Band Administrators, Chief and Council and the community are then determined by these colonial factors and we judge one another as 'indian' people as a consequence of a system devised by the European. In terms of cultural appropriation, and voice appropriation, the act of respecting the place of origin of a people/person is extremely valid, not just for 'authenticity' of what is a 'real indian', but as a defense mechanism. This process rightfully belongs in the hands of Indigenous people, and not in the hands of the colonizer (as it has been. The right to determine who is and isn't Indigenous should be the decision of each community and based on whichever criteria they decide, not indian Act policies. At the same time we must recognize which policies originate from colonial mind-sets and which we as Indigenous communities perpetuate. Current policy enables people who have not lived as, or who have not known themselves as Indigenous to easily claim that identity and to appropriate that voice and space. This is problematic. There becomes an expected and fixed principle of "Indian'ness" to abide and live by. This is an issue that needs further examining. A balance must be sought or strived towards.

The 'Indian-scale.'

In 'indian country' it is called the 'indian scale'. The scale determines how 'indian' you are. In one sense it is a paradox. It is used for irony and humour. In another sense, for those who are beginning to understand the politics of 'indianess', it can be harmful and a psychological whirlwind. It is harmful in the sense that individuals are seduced by the 'ideology' they choose to hail. In the process they become subject to that specific role and constrain themselves within this 'unrealistic', and perhaps superficial idea or notion of what it is to be an 'Indian'.

Another contradictory point to this is that the idea of the 'indian' is one based on the white-gaze, or the 'Hollywood-indian,' a 'fluffs n' feathers' indian.' This view of the 'indian' goes beyond aesthetic appearance, stereotypical notions of Aboriginal cosmology, or general notions of 'our' beliefs. 'indian'ness' becomes expected "ways of thinking, seeing, talking, being, acting," There are expected and fixed principles to abide by. All of these aforementioned aspects have roots in colonialism. Consequently the once oppressed person becomes an oppressor in the defining of who is and isn't an 'indian.' We begin to 'police' one another. We in turn carry out the process the dominant society has set in motion for us. The irony is that we, in turn, become part of that process and guilty of perpetuating it.

One specific experience comes to mind (in this determination of: "How Indian are you?") I was drinking with a group of *Anishnaabe-nini* (men) and three other *kwe* (women) one evening a few years ago. Perhaps before I engage in the story of the incident, I would like to explain where I am coming from. I am a Saulteau woman. I also have a Francophone father. I was raised in a northern Saulteau 'bush' environment. Our sense of 'traditional' of which we did not determine as "traditional" at that time is our language, knowledge, skills, and practises out on the land. Our spiritual practises were ones that occurred in our daily interactions with people, animals and the land. It was also mixed with Catholicism.

I am one who insists upon my mixed-blood identity. I must. There are several reasons for this. First, I am proud of and respect both cultural lenses that I was born into. I cannot and will not deny the blood of either of my ancestral lineage, nor should I be expected to. I have the 'full-blood' determinant weighing against me. My blood quantum will always be measured to that of the 'full blood.' I am expected to explain my political position and world-view. People find it even more precarious and interesting thus enjoy forcing me to choose one race over the other. I refuse. I have an Indigenous mind-set and world-view with franco mixed-blood running through my veins.

On this certain evening I believe my boldness and openness and my confidence with my mixed blood identity bothered a few individuals who have their own

127

"indian" identity issues. I was asked by an *Anishnaabe-nini* to choose one identity. He said I had to. I could not be both. Either you are or you aren't! Since this evening, I have heard similar analogies to this very situation. It is also similar to the "indian" expression of it not being possible to have a foot in each canoe. It became an argument. I refused to choose between identities. I kept repeating that I am both Saulteau and French. He continued to yell his question in my face, only getting louder. (I think he thought if he said it louder I would hear him better and understand him) I understood him all too well! I refused to choose, until our argument was out of control. He was screaming! He was demanding an answer, but my response was not an option. I had to choose. In frustration, I broke down into tears. I do come from an Indigenous reality, I am Saulteau, but I am also French and I refuse to deny this aspect of my father. Although I do not identify with my respective French culture I am from the blood of both cultures, bi-cultural. That particular evening I told him what he wanted to hear. He wanted me to be "indian" and nothing else. I never before had to defend nor prove my "indian" identity. I simply was who I was. A Saulteau-Cree/Franco woman. Well, it happens in our own communities. The irony is that it's our own people who are the 'police.' The oppressed become the oppressors, and colonialism continues to constrain and control us all.

The 'indian-scale' consists of some of these factors Where do you come from? Are you on-reserve, or off-reserve? Do you know your language? Are you learning your language? Do you dance pow-wow? Are you competition or traditional? Can you make bannock? Can you make moccasins? Can you sew? So are you a mixed-blood? Are you a C-31er? Do you have status? Are you Métis? Do you have your rights? Are you sponsored, or not? Are you an urban Indian? Were you adopted out?

These questions grow directly from European imperialistic definitions of 'indianness' from the Modernist Western Binary/Positional Thinking and the questions asked are examples of different determinants that can be and that are used in defining and judging how 'Indian' you are? Perhaps some of these determinants help us in identifying us as distinct Indigenous Peoples. Perhaps the questions are asked to understand where each of us comes from. They protect us. These questions (binaries) also work against us. These binaries that hail us, 'that seduce us' are used as a power gauge to separate us as Indigenous Peoples. It is part of a process that feeds into the 'malarkey' and chaos of the larger society's Ideological State Apparatuses: Ideas and images conveyed through radio, television and film; institutional education systems, at the elementary, junior and post-secondary level etc.; religious institutions and organizations; social welfare systems and so-called 'community relief or liaison.' The so called 'correctional' facilities and 'rehabilitation' systems or programs.

The protocol and determining of a person's 'indian'ness,' continues to cause many harmful variables. Another example of both the loss and the contradictory gaining of identity and rights is revealed in the outlandish irony and problematics that emerged because of the disenfranchisement and then, later, the reinstatement of "indian" status to women. The process of disenfranchising "indian" women when they married non-indian men reflects the ridiculous abuse of power that the colonial Canadian government has savoured over the past hundreds of years, and continue to hold under its colonial regime being dictated by Indian Act policies. Indigenous women lost their status and rights when they married non-Native men. They were also unable to pass on the special status and rights as an 'indian,' person to their children according to The Indian Act. These definitions of who and who isn't an 'indian' according to The Federal Government are not as important as the physical aspect of forced removal of Aboriginal women from our communities. The consequences have been the loss of ties and of the right to live on our ancestral land or with the community of our relatives, our family, our home, and even more so, the right to be buried in our ancestral territory with our ancestors. The irony of this situation is that non-Aboriginal women who married Aboriginal men were granted the rights and status that their female 'indian' counter-parts lost.

I am a product of this system. I have Indian Act policies limiting me whenever I choose to legally access rights from my Band. These legal definitions are not what form my notion of my 'Indian-essence.' However these protocols and policies infringe upon my life. My mother regained her status with the implementation of Bill C-31. Despite these changes, I, as a qualifier under Bill C-31, do not have access to the same rights and privileges as a 'full-blood' indian, nor do I have access to the same rights than an "indian" man may pass on to both his white wife and his "mixed-blood" children. His wife and children carry more rights and privileges than a reinstated Indigenous woman and her "mixed-blood" children through Bill C-31. Bill C-31 was not an act that ended discrimination in our communities. Rather it was an act to provide a short term solution to 'gender' discrimination of that era, now the second generation offspring (known as Bill C-31ers), suffer the consequences. My children (if I marry a non-Indigenous man) will not receive any status and rights of recognition as an 'indian' person according to the Indian Act and The Federal Government. Thankfully, the Indian Act does not and will not determine nor dictate the cultural lens of my children and their children. My children, despite their blood quantum, will carry my Saulteau "mixed-blood" lens, knowledge, language and world-view.

I am relieved because my notion of myself as an Indigenous person does not solely grow out of the Indian Act. It is infringed upon, and at times forces me to identify. It would be sad for our communities if the Indian Act provided the only basis of our identity. If we are to choose to abide by the dominant structure's ideologies, then this would be the only affirmation and validity of determining our 'indianness.'

The policies that grow out of a colonial government, cause divisions in Band Council politics and deeper divisions within the community. We in the end, focus upon such frivolous power struggles, while overlooking larger daunting issues outside of this.

A closing....

The three differing examples of ideologically influenced situations are complicated and are rooted in colonial beliefs. It becomes difficult to identify what is and isn't relevant or what 'really' pertains to us as Indigenous Peoples since ideologies surround us. In regards to the colonial situation. We must as

Indigenous and non-Indigenous thinkers develop different paradigms, 'ways of seeing' or interpreting the impact of contact, conquest and colonialism. We must strive to create and continue building the Indigenous discourse and narrative that has always existed since "time immemorial."

The three different experiences shed light on the complications of 'indian identity' and the hurt and pain that we as Indigenous Peoples are affected by in almost every facet of our lives. As Indigenous Peoples, we are born into this constructed "indian" ideology that is established by the dominant society and it becomes perpetuated by individuals who are hailed by the ideologies even to those who refuse to identify 'consciously,' with these ideologies. However, we are all affected by these "indian" constructs, even those individuals who think they are by their own free will defining themselves, they are also being hailed in some manner by the concepts, language and ideas that we choose. All these are upheld by the dominant culture who looks to explain and interpret our representation as "indian" People. We are part of this ideological process and perpetrators of it.

It is this process of critical and honest reflection concerning the actualization of colonization and the process of assimilation that is liberating. According to Terry Eagleton it involves, "the most difficult of all forms of liberation: freeing ourselves from ourselves." (Eagleton, 1999:58) My understanding of what Eagleton means is that by consciously critiquing and analysing how ideologies work to process themselves in our individual lives and particular experiences we free ourselves. We can then begin to engage in a self-analytical reflection process of actualization and which is thus a "tool" in the process of liberation and breakdown of ideology in our lives and as a collective of Indigenous Peoples.

Once we begin to honestly recognize the colonial images and ideologies that we are saturated within we can begin to take back the power and discourse to reclaim who we are as Indigenous People. We do this so that we are not simply "surviving as indians." In an attempt to move beyond living in defiance and resistance to the dominant societies' constructed "indian" ideologies, to what we dream ourselves to be as differing Indigenous nations of People.

Author's Note:

This paper grew out of a second year level course. It was both my first and last "Post-colonial theory" class. One that I survived. Although I agree with the intention of deconstruction, I do not adhere to the misused and romantic notion of the term "post-colonial." To ascribe to this belief would be to support a farce. We as Indigenous people continue to struggle to remedy this attack of genocide on a daily basis. If we lived in Post-colonial times, then we as Indigenous Peoples would be more harmonious, rich(er), healthier people. We would have fewer qualms to hash-out with the government and dominant society. Perhaps we would posses a few miles of land (that is actually arable) to feed our babies. We would definitely be a happier bunch of "indians" wouldn't we?

Bibliography

Alexie, Sherman. (1994). The Lone Ranger and Tonto Fistfight in Heaven. New York: Harper Perrenial.

Althusser, Louis. "Louis Althusser from "Ideology and Ideological State Apparatuses," (1970) A Critical and Cultural Theory Reader, Eds. Anthony Easthope and Kate McGowan (Toronto: University of Toronto Press, 1922) 51-57.

hooks, bell. "Theory as Liberatory Practise." Teaching to Transgress: Education as The Practise of Freedom (London: Routledge, 1994), 59-75

Said, Edward W. "Orientalism" The Post-Colonial Studies Reader eds. Bill Ashcroft, Gareth Griffiths, Helen Griffiths, Helen Tiffin (London: Routledge, 1995) 87-92

Notes: "Modernist Western Binary Thinking" (Molly Blyth, Native Studies 230:1999.)

Notes: "Some Preliminary Notes On Althusser's Ideology and Ideological State Apparatuses: (Molly Blyth, Native Studies 230: 1999)

Valaskakis, Gail Guthrie. "Post-cards of my Past". Relocating Cultural Studies. Eds. Valda Blundell, John Sheperd and Ian Taylor (London: 1993). 155-70

GEARY HOBSON

LIVE COVERAGE OF THE INDUCTION CEREMONIES AT THE INAUGURATION OF THE SERIAL KILLERS
HALL OF FAME

Good evening, fans from all across America. I'm Harv Flippin, along with Buzz
Brinkley, coming to you live from the Christopher Wilder Auditorium in beautiful
Pompano Beach, Florida, bringing you the entire program of the induction
ceremonies for the inauguration of the Serial Killers Hall of Fame. This is truly,
truly, an auspicious occasion. The air is simply crackling with excitement, with
tension, and now, just minutes away from the opening ceremonies, people are
still filing into the auditorium. I believe it can truly be said, Buzz, that we are
witnessing history in the making."

"No doubt about it, Harv. I know that I am, and I know that you, too, are highly,
highly honoured to be here broadcasting this momentous event. And good
evening to you, sports fans, I'm sure you're going to enjoy this stupendous event
just as much as Harv and I will enjoy bringing it to you."

"Thank you, Buzz, for those most gracious and lofty thoughts."

Voice now lowered, a decibel or two in respect to the preponderance to come.

"Fans, who would have thought, only one year ago, that we would now be
opening a Hall of Fame for Serial Killers. So long talked about, so long dreamed
of, but now, thanks to so many dedicated, truly visionary individuals and
corporations, we can now not only announce that our finest and most dedicated
serial killers are finally getting their just due, but we can now actually televise the
complete induction ceremonies as we open the Hall to the world-at-large. We

have our Baseball Hall of Fame, our Basketball Hall of Fame and Football Hall of Fame, and I might add, both for collegiate and professional athletes, and there are Halls of Fame for tennis, and golf and auto racing. There are Halls of rock'n roll musicians, for aviation pioneers, for businessmen, for cowboys and Indians, but until now, there hasn't been one for the nation's—indeed, the world's fastest growing sport—serial killing."

Turning back to Buzz, Harv intones: "And now, Buzz, we're entering a new era. Serial killers have indeed come into their own."

"Yes, Harv, and high time, I say. And, Harv, I think we should take our hats off to such far-seeing organizations as the National Rifle Association—incidentally, our premier sponsor for this momentous event—in helping to bring the Hall into reality."

"Well put, Buzz. It goes without saying that the NRA, ever the great guardian of our individual liberties as Americans, has been of immeasurable benefit to the great sport of serial-killing, in so many ways."

"Harv, I hear there's a small protest group outside, demanding among many things, that the Hall not be allowed to open. They say that attention given to such people as serial killers does more than just perpetuate the phenomenon—that it actually encourages the sport."

"Yes, Buzz, I'm not at all surprised. There's always such kooks who feel they have to protest everything. Well, rest assured, Buzz. They'll never get inside. Security is beefed up all around. Our brave boys in blue will make sure that only the right people get in, no victim's rights groups, no pissed-off (Oops, excuse me, heh heh heh) surviving family members, no burned-out homicide detectives get in to disrupt this truly auspicious occasion."

"Harv, I'm getting a report from Gina Groopie, our roving reporter on the auditorium floor. She tells me that Charlton Heston and Rush Limbaugh are in attendance. She says that Rush says he wouldn't miss this event for the world."

"Great, Buzz. And say, will you look at all those banners down there ? Some of those contingent's are really going all out for their favourites. Look: There's the Ted Bundy delegation—TED BUNDY WHAT A GUY! And, how about that sign—GET DEAD FOR TED. And that one—BUNDY, BUNDY/HE'LL EVEN DO YOU ON A SUNDAY. Now that's clever. You know, Buzz, it's really great to see all this spirit being shown for the fine sport—art, even—of serial killing."

"Right you are, Harv. And how about the Gerald Stano delegation? A great turn-out for another local favourite son. Just look at those signs: STANO-CAN-O and JERRY'S THE ONE and SHORT-ORDER COOKS FOR STANO."

"No question about it, Buzz. The stakes are high, and each group is going all out for its own favourite. But, now, Buzz, I think we need to inform our viewing audience about the procedures and protocol for induction into the Hall. Who gets in and how they get in. I know our viewers are anxious to know how things are cooking."

"Yes, Harv, I believe you're right." *Turning slightly sideways to face the camera face-forward.* "Ladies and gentleman, the procedures for induction into the Hall of Fame are actually quite simple. The Serial Killers Archives, maintained by journalists who have written extremely fascinating and ground breaking stories on serial killer activities and also of selected capital criminal defense lawyers, conducts a vote by mail. The Archives, I might add, is funded by that great beacon of journalistic endeavour, *The American Enquirer*, and is located right here in beautiful Pompano Beach. The mail vote, and this of course is the first year it has been in place, asks members to vote for five candidates for selection in this inaugural effort. The balloting has been conducted, and the results are secreted in one of Price Waterhouse's inestimable vaults, even as we speak."

"Thank you, Buzz. I couldn't have said it better myself." *Turning toward the camera full face-forward.* "And now, my fellow sports enthusiasts, who will these five pioneering personalities be? Can we just speculate for a moment, mull the immense possibilities, indulge our fantasies, or shall we merely sit back and wait for the magic moment when the master of ceremonies shall make the astounding announcements?"

"Oh, Harv, I think we owe it to our audience. Let's speculate, let's—oh, by the way, who is the MC for this evening's gala celebration?"

"Why, Buzz, none other than the incomparable Johnny Cochran himself. Old Mr. Get-em-Off-At-All-Costs himself."

"That's outstanding, Harv. Imagine-Johnny Cochran. Wow!"

"Yes, Buzz. Now, who do you think has the best chance for election this year, do you care to go on record at this early stage of the festivities?"

"Well, Harv", *ponderously, deliberately.* "Since you put me on the spot—heh, heh, I'll go out on the old proverbial limb and declare that Ted Bundy will definitely be a first-time electee. And, Harv, I even predict he'll be a unanimous choice on all the voters' ballots."

"Now, Buzz. That's not going out on the old limb all that much. I mean, you know—Ted Bundy! Why, just look what he's done for the sport."

"Yes, Harv. I know. That's why I place him at the top of my list. You know, others might have chalked up higher kill counts, or operated for a longer period of time, but Ted—"

"Indeed, one can't deny that of all who have practised the fine craft of serial killing, that Ted Bundy undoubtedly deserves election into the Hall because of his sheer brilliance, his dash, his charisma, *savoir faire*."

"*Savoir faire*, yes. Yes, Harv. There's Jack the Ripper. There's the Green River

Guy. There's the Hillside fellows. There's that charming rascal Henry Lee Lucas. But, you know, Harv. There's only one Ted."

"You said it, Buzz."

"Right, Harv. It's like the old adage: a Ford is a car, but a Cadillac is a Cadillac. Well, I believe it can truly be said that just as Gerry Stano is a serial killer, Jerome Brudos is a serial killer, Westley Dodd is a serial killer, that Ted is a Ted!"

"Exactly, Buzz. I ask you: who in the twentieth century has brought so much to the fine sport of serial killing? Those good looks, that impish, boyish smile. And, you know, Buzz, it's been said that all his victims felt it was an honour to be done by Ted."

"Yes, as well they should feel honoured, Harv."

"Well, I think we're both in agreement that Ted Bundy will probably most definitely be on the Hallowed List of Five."

"Harv, pardon me for digressing for a moment, but don't you think we should allow our viewers to see some of the convention floor while you and I speculate on the electees?"

"Great idea, Buzz. We'll just have the cameramen pan the audience below, try to give all you wonderful viewers out there in TV land a close-up of what's shaking here at Chris Wilder Auditorium. Guys, can you pan the crowd below? Thanks a bunch."

"Look at all those signs, Harv. Look over there! There appears to be a large bloc of supporters for Jeffery Dahmer: HANDSOME JEFF—HE'S READY TO DEVOUR YOU WITH REAL MAN LOVE. And how about that one for heroic John Wayne Gacy: GIVE ME YOUR BOYS AND I'LL SHOW YOU WHAT I CAN DO WITH THEM. It certainly appears the gay contingent isn't going to be left out, doesn't it? And over there, Harv. Supporters for Westley Dodd, and Dean Corll, and rugged, burly Bob Burdella. Yes, the gays are certainly making themselves heard."

"As indeed they should, Buzz. It all goes to prove how very, very democratic serial-killing really is." *Intensely, intimately.* "As a matter of fact, this leads us back to our principal topic—who will be tonight's premier inductees? I think, Buzz, that a true spirit of ecumenicity will prevail all across the board, with the electees coming from all walks of life, all races, both sexes, and every sexual persuasion."

"So, Harv. Do I take it that you're ready to venture a guesstimate as to who our five inductees will be this evening?"

"Yes, Buzz. I believe I'm prepared to do just that." *Turning face-forward to the battery of the cameras.* "It is my judgment that tonight's honourees will be—are you ready? One, Ted Bundy. Two, Ronnie Reagan for his humanitarian, off-the-field efforts toward the encouragement and growth of the sport—and Buzz, this will set a precedent. I predict that each year, we'll see the induction of a judge who let a serial killer squeak by, to fall conveniently through the cracks, so to speak; or an enterprising cop in the precinct, like those wide-awake and far-seeing cops in Seattle and San Diego who allowed the Green River Killer—or Greenie, as he is now affectionately known—and Eddie Cole, go free through convenient relaxing of their duties. Three, Richard Ramirez, the creepy, crazy L.A. Night Stalker, as a token appreciation of our minorities. And, Buzz, let's don't forget the gals: I predict Arlene Wuornos will make it. As we've already discussed it, minorities and women represent very important constituencies in the sport. And five, Ed Gein, the Wisconsin killer of the 40s and 50s, who'll go into the Hall via the Veteran's Committee vote.

"Ed Gein, Harv? Not Jack the Ripper?"

"No, Buzz. Quite simply, this is not Jack's year. And here are my reasons for this conclusion. One, Eddie Gein has recently come into his own with the popularity of *The Silence of the Lambs*, in which the killer depicted therein is based partially on Eddie. Two, the Brits are currently undergoing a great deal of loss of popularity world wide, Buzz, and I seriously believe this will have an adverse effect on Jack's chances for election."

"My goodness! And do you believe this will prevail for sometime to come, Harv?"

"Yes, Buzz. I'm afraid that such worthies as Peter Sutcliffe—the old Yorkshire Ripper himself—and Reginald Christie and others will be left waiting in the wings for quite some time to come. Now, of course, if a new serial killer should suddenly pop up in such an unriveting place as Wales or Stoke-on-Kent, why, then that might refocus America's, and, indeed, the entire world's attention, once more on the Brits."

"This is really eye-opening, Harv."

"Thank you, Buzz. And you know, Buzz? The real key to a serial killer's image, his popularity, is a catchy, zippy name. That's the key. The Green River Killer, the Boston Strangler, the Freeway Killer, The Hillside Strangler, the Night Stalker, the Southside Slayer—and, you know, Buzz? Where would we be without our journalists? I mean, you know these guys are something else. It takes a great deal of—well, imagination—to come up with those snazzy names, all of which goes so far in making our sport the colourful pastime that it is."

"Yes, Harv. I totally agree. And don't you think that there should be a journalists' wing of the Hall—like they have for broadcasters at Cooperstown?"

"Exactly, Buzz. That's an idea that will most certainly become an eventuality, I lay you odds. But getting back to our possible inductees. What do you think of the Green River Killer's chances, Buzz?"

"Well, now, Harv, Greenie has brought a certain—how shall we say it? a *je ne sais quois*, to the sport. He's creepy. No one knows to this day, who he—or they—is, or are. And, one might venture to hope—his total is possibly still mounting. Isn't it forty-nine now, and counting? No, Harv, we still have to consider Greenie among the actives and therefore not yet eligible for election. But his day will come."

"Yes, no doubt about it, Buzz. Greenie's dominating presence in the sport has certainly been felt, and I'll be the first to admit that we all—fans and participants alike—owe a great debt of gratitude to Greenie. However, and this must be said in all candor, you've got to admit that Greenie's clientele—when we compare them to Ted's sorority girls and All-American beauties—doesn't rank him in Ted's category, or even in charming Chris Wilder's either. I mean, street-hookers? Come on now! Greenie's targets are always low priority and easily obtainable—not like the bold venturings of Ted or Chris into sorority dorms or abducting single preoccupied girls searching for their car keys in parking lots of suburban shopping malls."

"Yes, I agree, Harv. Hookers are notoriously low-profile. Especially street-hookers. They are the absolute bottom of the barrel, and they have always been easy marks for the hunter."

"Yes, Buzz. Even an amateur sportsman could bag one. Street-hookers merely give a bad name, and an even worse image, to prostitution in general. A far cry from the glamour of *Pretty Woman*. Now there's a movie!"

"You know, Harv. We mustn't overlook the minorities. And women, too! Look at the support delegation down below for Arlene Wuormos—another local favourite. Look at that sign, ARLENE: A GIRL FOR ALL SEASONS and that one: ARLENE MAKES BACON OUT OF (MC) PIGS"

"Yes, Buzz. I believe that Arlene is a definite shoo-in as one of the five as yet unknown inductees. And look over there, still scanning the minority entries, a sizeable bloc in support of Wayne Williams, the Atlanta Child Killer, and also over there, one for Richard Ramirez, the L.A. Night Stalker. But you know, Buzz, I'm a little surprised there isn't a bigger turnout for Juan Corona, who did so much fine work in Northern California in the early 70s."

"Well, Harv, that's part of the reason. It was so long ago, and the voters probably assume his candidacy belongs to the Veteran's Committee, and when you're up against such heavy-weights of the past, like Jack the Ripper and Al Fish and Herman Webster Mudgett—not to mention such long ago worthies as Gilles de Rais, Shaka, Heinrich Himmler, Timothy McVeigh."

"Now, Buzz, you're beginning to veer off into the domain of the mass murderer, departing, however slightly, from the career and purview of the serial killer per se."

"Yes, Harv, I know." *Buzz begins, very ponderous, intellectually deliberative.* "But you know, Harv?, and sports fans, somewhere down the road the Powers That Be are going to have to develop some clearer guide lines concerning the all-important distinctions between bona fide serial killers and mass murderers. At this extreme, it's like comparing Tolstoy and T.S. Eliot with Louis L'Amour and Rod McKuen."

"Oh, Buzz, you over-intellectualizing son-of-a-gun! Tolstoy and Eliot—my goodness! But, you know, you're right, old pal. A line must be drawn. For one thing, the serial killer is a true artist, but a mass murderer is a journeyman."

"Well, it's obvious that the answer is a separate Hall of Fame for Mass Murderers."

"Buzz, I understand it's already in the works. Philanthropists and planners at Idi Amin University, in coordination with Dr. Samuel Thugg-Hammer of the Population Erasure Studies Department at Chivington University, are, even as we speak, submitting finalized plans for just such an institution."

"Wonderful! Truly wonderful."

"And, you know, Buzz", *Harv is reflective, speaking quietly in hushed tones.* "It's probably safe to say that there's most likely, right at this very moment, hundreds of little Ted Bundys and Jerry Stanos out there, watching our broadcast, dreaming of what they will eventually become."

"How edifying, Harv. I don't think I could have said it better myself."

"But, you know, Buzz, I was just thinking. Have you noticed lately that Ted Bundy has been receiving all sorts of adverse criticism, some people saying that he whined and cried like a baby just before his execution, that he was bargaining for more time with investigating detectives about his actual body count and such even up to the time they threw the switch. I'm just hopeful that this negativity will not adversely affect his election into the Hall."

"Not a chance, Harv. I think Ted has an absolute lock on it."

"Oh, Buzz. I have a flash from Gina down below on the convention floor. There's heavy speculation that former President Reagan will most likely be one of this evening's inductees, and that he might even make a surprise visit to the auditorium."

"Wow! Is that right?"

"Outstanding! It'll be great to see Ronnie in public again. And, you know, Buzz, it's entirely fitting that he be honoured as well as all those heroic guys out there in the field, so to speak, doing the child raping and killing, the prostitute-strangling, the coed stalkers and slashers, but, you know, we mustn't forget all those dedicated individuals who work behind the scenes—all the paid psychiatrists, the defence attorneys, the tolerant judges, who do so much to help our serial killers flourish in this democratic society of ours. So, without a doubt, and with not a smidgin of compunction at all, I say that Ronnie Reagan should get his due. All that bold cutting back of costly mental health programs, the closing of unnecessary, duplicative hospitals and sanatoriums, Ronnie, in his quiet and heroic way, made it possible for the Henry Lucases and David Carpenters and Arthur Shawcrosses that we've come to so love and admire, to flourish, truly nascent exotic flowers blooming out of the soil of mental healthdom."

"Harv, what you've just said is so moving."

"You really think so, Buzz?"

"I surely do, Harv."

"Well, big guy, I'm sure you're right. And, you know, it doesn't look like we will have much longer to wait—but, hold it, Buzz. I have a flash from Gina Groopie, our roving girl reporter."

"Put her on live, fellas."

"Harv, Buzz. This is Gina down below."

"Yes, Gina. What do you have for us?"

"Guys, there's a minor foul up with the overhead news liner. Do you see what I'm talking about?"

"Yes, Gina. What's it saying?"

"Oh, my God, Harv. Just read what it says: SERIAL KILLERS ARE NOT HOTHOUSE ORCHIDS, EXOTIC AND BEAUTIFUL—THEY ARE SHIT-IMBIBING AND SCUM-SWILLING POISONOUS MUSHROOMS SPAWNED OUT OF THE DETRITUS OF DEBASING POVERTY, UNBRIDLED CHILD ABUSE, AND ABJECT PARENTAL NEGLECT. Oh, my God, Harv, it's probably those spoil sports from the National Organization for Victim Abuse or the National Center for Missing and Exploited Children or some such. A fine time for them to show up."

"Yes, indeed, Buzz. I surely hope that Pompano Beach's finest puts the kibosh to their shenanigans."

"And, yes, Harv. Just as we speak, there they are, the brave boys in blue, up in the control booth, and bingo! There goes the tiresome propaganda."

"Thank heavens for the local *gendarmerie*, Buzz. Now maybe we can have a beautiful uneventful ceremony to honour our great."

"Yes, Harv, and now, can you please add a bit more about the other potential inductees, and of the wonderful sport that we are all here to honour and, dare I say it, even perpetuate?"

"Why, of course, Buzz. I'll continue my remarks *apres* Ted. You know, Buzz, and sports fans all across America, serial killing, despite the current popular attention it is so deservedly receiving, didn't just begin in the last twenty years. No, it has been around for quite a long while—of course, Jack the Ripper in 1880s London, and Herman Webster Mudgett about the same time in Chicago and Toronto are early examples of the particular modern-day sort of finesse that goes a long way toward making the pastime the truly remarkable activity that we know it to be today. But much further back, when our great American nation was forming, there were early practitioners even then. There was intrepid Lewis Wetzel, stalking and killing Shawnee redskins on the Virginia frontier. And Tom Quick, the Delaware Killer; and Liver-Eating Johnston, the Crow Killer; and history has it that even old Daniel Boone himself got in his licks with some occasional redskin stalking. Why, it might even be said that serial killing is the American Way. However, even that statement, should I choose to halt my remarks at this point, would be inaccurate, because serial killing goes even further back, way back into the very bowels of Western Civilization. Why, even the mythic forerunners of Dracula style vampires, as well as werewolves, and succubi and incubi, and lamias and witches of all kinds, might even be regarded as the predecessors to today's Ted Bundys, David Berkowitzes, John Wayne Gacys and Stephen Pennells. No, fans, maybe even Cain himself went on to polish off other brothers and sisters—who can tell? Serial killing is immeasurably old, almost as old as mankind itself. But in the last decade, what with new technological and psychiatric advances, the sport has truly blossomed. Where once a Liver-Eating Johnston was simply a stalking killer of redskins—uhh, heh heh, Native Americans—a modern-day Ted Bundy or Bob Burdella is a true artiste. It all just goes to illustrate how the sport has truly flourished in recent times."

"Wow, Harv. That's quite a speech. I couldn't have said it better myself. You know, you've really put the whole thing onto an extraordinary lofty and thought-provoking perspective."

"Thank you, Buzz. That was indeed my intention." *Harv basks in the limelight briefly, looking solemnly into the camera, then turns his attention to his partner.* "Now, Buzz, I believe our grand evening is about to get underway. I see Johnny Cochran approaching center stage. Yes, indeed, we are getting underway!" *A huge fanfare of music bursts forth, which is quickly recognizable as the opening barrage of Richard Strauss' Thus Spake Zarathustra. Cochran, immaculately clad in a tuxedo, stands before a podium, empowered by the latest in microphone technology. As Strauss' eye-opening and ear-numbing crescendo dies away, Cochran holds his arms aloft to stem the audience's thunderous applause.*

"Thank you, ladies and gentlemen. Thank you. Thank you. Welcome to the Christopher Wilder Auditorium in beautiful Pompano Beach, Florida, where we are all of us witnesses to a momentous occasion in our illustrious nation's history. Tonight we inaugurate the Serial Killers Hall of Fame. I know this is an event you've all been waiting for. Thanks to such intrepid sponsors as the National Rifle Association, the American Tobacco Company, Prudential Life, and literally dozens more whose honoured names will be mentioned more than once throughout the evening, we who are in the forefront of the new field of Judicio-Sports are honoured to take part in this stupendous occasion." *Clearing his throat slightly and adjusting his black bow tie, he continues his remarks.*

"In a few moments, the introduction of our first inductee will be announced, but first, a message from one of our many splendid sponsors." *The Strauss extravaganza blares forth again. A commercial is aired and Cochran again comes to fore.* "And now, ladies and gentlemen"—*and he bows, clapping his*

145

hands, while stepping back a pace or two, and a troop of dancers, eight white college girl-types, clad in short skirts, tennis shoes, and heavy pullovers emblazoned with various Greek letters indicating sororities. All the girls wear their hair long, parted in the middle, and they begin a lively shuffle while singing:
I yearn to know
A boy named Ted.
He stalks the campus
To make me dead.

Buzz and Harv come back into the picture.

"No surprise here, is there, Harv? I guess we know who the first inductee will be."

"I agree, Buzz. But now, I believe we need to explain Johnny's reference to Judicio-Sports. Some of our viewers might not be familiar with the term."

"Right, Harv. Judicio Sports is indeed a new concept, and Johnny Cochran is an excellent representative of the enterprise. It's divided into several divisions, all designed to propel legal matters into spectator sportsdom—lawyers who intrepidly battle to win at all costs—and Johnny and his colleague Alan Dershowitz are, at this point, the virtual Muhammad Alis and Mike Tysons of their field. There's consulting psychiatrists and psychologists who likewise do their humanly best to spring their clients. There's the judges category but wait, we're running out of time, and so we now switch you back to Johnny Cochran."

All attention is once again focussed on Cochran at center stage as he makes a short introduction of the first presentation, an actor who gained fame for playing psychopathic killers. Very smoothly, the handsome man produces an envelope from the inside pocket of his tuxedo, opens it with a flourish, and quietly intones: "Ted Bundy."

The applause is thunderous, the Ted girls once again troop out on stage, orchestral music rises to its customary crescendo. As the noise subsides, Johnny

Cochran reads a brief summary of Bundy's life and exploits: his emergence from humble surroundings in the Pacific Northwest, his struggles as a law student, his near-impossible maintenance of cover as a law student, and Republican party gopher while quietly developing and then plying his craft as a serial killer. The audience is in throes of ecstasy. Then the auditorium darkens, brief film clips of episodes of Ted Bundy's life are played, accompanied by a delightful rendition of "A Boy Named Ted." As the short five minute cinematic party ends, an organ segues into the soundtrack, intoning a deeply churchy chorale, "Sheep May Safely Graze."

"Harv," Buzz whispers. "Gina down below on the auditorium floor has another report. Wow! Whaddya know? Gina says that, even as we speak, a fledgling serial killer has just made public a note saying he gets off on snuffing news media personnel."

"No kidding? That's highly original. Put Gina on live, on the overhead, so all our viewing audience can hear her report first-hand."

"Harv? Buzz? Can you hear me? This is Gina. Gina Groopie reporting live from the convention floor. Yes, it's true. We've just received a hand-written note from a person who states he is a beginning serial killer. He says he's to be known as Newsnuffer, and that he's debuting here tonight, and that he expects fair and impartial coverage."

"Newsnuffer? Wow, Gina, that's clever and catchy. Tell me, Gina, have you met him yet? Can you get an interview?"

"No, Buzz, I haven't met him yet, and yes, I will try for an interview."

Now Johnny Cochran is back on the podium, announcing the next inductee. Wayne Williams' selection brings a surge of applause.

"Harv?" Buzz whispers off camera. "I've just received word that Arlene Wuornos, Ed Gein, and former President Reagan are definitely the next three inductees."

"Outstanding! Well, we'll keep it to ourselves."

"Harv? Buzz? Gina again. There's a report that a photo journalist from *The American Enquirer* has been found in the back row of the auditorium, strangled with an electrical cord, and there's a note pinned to his shirt collar containing only the word "Newssnuffer.""

"My goodness! So his career is really on its' way! Gina, try for that interview!"

"Will do, Harv. I'll get back to you and—Aaawhkk! Guhhkk!"

"What was that last, Gina? I didn't quite catch it."

"Harv? Did you see that? On the monitor. Gina just suddenly disappeared! It looked like something grabbed her by the neck! She was there one second, and then the next, she was gone!"

"Buzz, find out what you can."

Buzz gets up and moves over to the cameramen facing them, but there are no cameramen there.

"Harv? The camera guys are gone! What the hell's going on? What's happening around here?" *Buzz turns back toward Harv, suddenly a black rubber rope in a loop encircles his neck, and he is pulled out of Harv's sight, screaming, and then finally ending with gross choking sounds.*

"My God, Buzz! Are you all right? Are you all right? Goddammit, what's going on?"

Down below, the auditorium is being quickly emptied by screaming people in tuxedos and evening dresses. Johnny Cochran, in the middle of reading a tribute to Arlene Wuornos, looks perplexed, like he's heard a rumour about a fire in the building without hearing the alarm.

Up above, in the play-by-play announcer's booth, Harv looks down at the rising pandemonium. He hears a slight noise behind him, but before he can turn around, his head is pulled back in a strong violent movement, and as he starts to mouth a loud protest, everything goes black.

ROBERTA KENNEDY

"LET ME TELL YOU A STORY OF MY PEOPLE"

I like to perform Haida songs and stories at potlatches, feasts, and for the general public, for elementary and high schools, for university classes and at storytelling festivals. I like to share this small part of my culture. It's important for me. It's important for my children. It's important for other people to know that we exist. I meet too many people who do not know the struggles Aboriginal Peoples went through to get where we are today. Don't get me wrong, I do not speak for all Aboriginal Peoples. I would not dare to do that. We are all individuals. I cannot even speak for all Haida people. I can only speak for myself on these issues that I wish to share with you. We, too, are individuals. We are not a group to be lumped together.

Let me tell you about the cultural work I do. My nickname is Roberta Kennedy. My real name, my Haida name is *Kwee-gay-ee-ones*. It means, "Big precious cloud" or "Big loved cloud." It was my grandmother's name on my mother's side. I am from two nations, Haida and Squamish. I know more about my Haida ancestry as I was born and raised on *Haida Gwaii* (literally, "The land of the good people"). Many know these islands as the Queen Charlotte Islands. The Haida practice a matrilineal tradition. The two main family groups, or clans, are passed down through the mother. These two main clans are the Ravens and Eagles. There are sub-clans as well, but I will not explain as it does get complicated. I belong to the Raven Clan, or the *Yagu-lanas* Clan.

The reason for the descent through the mother is because the woman is considered to be the strongest. She is the one who carries the babies. She is the centre of the home. In our clans we have matriarchs. The oldest woman in our clans has the most power. She is the mother and grandmother and great-grandmother of us all. For this reason, we call her, *Naanii* (grandmother). She has all of the wisdom. We go to her for answers, for guidance. To be a woman, at least with the Haida people, is a good thing. I feel very lucky.

But, on the other hand, I am not so lucky. My people have a history of misfortune. To give you the full picture, I have to go back over a hundred years. Before contact with Europeans, our islands were populated with villages all up and down *Haida Gwaii*. After contact, our populations were decimated by ninety percent due to the smallpox epidemic. But, we survived. My great-great-aunt Florence Edenshaw told of her mother (my great-great-great-grandmother, Isabella) getting saved from the smallpox epidemic. Some of her uncles came in a canoe to the village. When they saw that smallpox was there, they grabbed Isabella and her aunt from the beach and left with them. Florence's great-grandfather had a gun and threatened the uncles with it. Isabella's sister, Wiba, was too far away to grab. Everyone in that village died, including Wiba. My great-great-great- grandmother lived because of this kidnapping, and I am grateful as I am here today with my own family of Raven children to prove it. Everything happens for a reason. *How'aa* (thank you) Creator.

After smallpox, missionaries were sent into our remaining villages to convert us to Christianity. The missionaries told our people that the rest of us would die unless we converted. Many were scared and they converted. All had to give up the traditional lifestyles. Then our Potlatches were banned. Some people were put in jail for Potlatching. Usually, at a Potlatch, a Chief would give away all his family had. Participating at Potlatches meant that a lot of school and church were missed. To change this, the missionaries petitioned the government to pass a law that would send the children to residential schools. In these schools, the priest and nuns believed that if the children learned English, then they would have succeeded, as they would be assimilated. Children all across North America were sent to these schools for ten months of every year. The schools were situated far from home, often a thousand kilometres away.

When I first moved to Edmonton, I met a Cree woman who had attended residential school in Alberta. She named some of the students she went to school with and I said, "Those people are some of my relatives. I didn't know they sent my people this far away." She hugged me really hard and said, "the schools touched all of our lives. They hurt all of us. It doesn't matter if you went or your grandparents went. It hurts us still." I wanted to cry, and I sometimes do. I wanted to be angry, but I am past this. I want to tell you about this so you know. It hurts me knowing the pain my family went through. It hurts me knowing there is a lot of pain my family is still going through.

Some of the children tried running away from these schools. They did this because these children, no matter the age, six years old, or ten years old, or sixteen years old, were severely punished. They were beaten for speaking their languages, they were made to feel ashamed of their Aboriginal ways, their very names were ridiculed. Many of these kids arrived at these schools speaking no English at all. This would mean that they would be beaten a lot until they started speaking English. Many children were sexually abused by the priests and nuns who were teaching them to be 'respectable human beings.'

These children were also starved. The food quality was very poor. My great-aunt tells of eating a lot of 'mush.' The bread was stale and the portions were small. In some cases I heard that the nuns and priests were on budgets, and couldn't afford better. But, I also heard that the nuns and priests received superior food, and were not in want. Some children would steal food whenever they could, to stave off hunger pangs. I could go on, but I will not as this could fill a book. It was the same all across Canada.

Many of these children returned to their villages, English speaking, with only a bit of schooling. Not a lot as they were put to work in these schools. My great-aunt Lavina told me that she spent half of the day cleaning and cooking before having some lessons in arithmetic, reading and writing. Naanii Lavina says, "My mother taught me everything I know. At school, all I learned was a little English."

This history has hurt us in many ways. We lost traditional medicines and our medicine people. We lost songs. We lost stories. We lost names. We lost lineages. Most importantly, we lost our language. My grandfather spoke an old Haida dialect. He didn't teach it to any of his ten children. He didn't want his children to be ridiculed for speaking an old-fashioned language. He was the last one to speak this dialect. And unfortunately, he died with our language locked in his tongue forever.

When I talk to groups of people, depending on the time I have been given, I share as much history as I can. I feel this is a very important part of getting people to understand who I am, and how I came to stand here before them. It is meant to let people know what happened to my people, and why we have problems today. This history clearly illustrates, for example, why I do not speak my own language.

I like to sing Haida songs to alleviate the heaviness that might accompany the information that I share in my presentations. I wish I could sing you a song today, but that will not translate in this essay. Maybe you will hear me perform one day. I can, however share a story that I frequently use when I perform.

This is a much shortened version of the story I tell. A special *judda* (woman) lived on *Haida Gwaii* thousands of years ago. She was kind, happy, beautiful, clever, helpful and generous. She went berry picking one day. While in the berry patch she remembered her *Naaniis* (grandmothers) telling her to sing to frighten the bears away. As she sang her song reached to the sky and beyond where the moon awoke. The moon smiled and thought about how wonderful her voice was and reached to pick her up. It would be an amazing thing if this *judda* could sing for the world to hear her and be happy that day. So now the woman becomes *Koon Judda* (woman in the moon). But, her people do not know this. And they cry as they believe she is dead, never to be seen or heard from again. They cry for many days. And as *Koon Judda* can hear them she aches to try and think of some way to ease their pain. Until she remembers the berries she brought to the moon and she tosses them across the night sky, where they become stars and all can look up and know that *Koon Judda* is watching over them all and singing her happy songs.

This is my favourite story. It is a crest, or symbol that has been sewn on to my button robe. My great-grandmother, Naanii Beatrice Brown, made my robe for me when I graduated from high school. This crest was her favourite. It is now mine. And my robe will now become an heirloom, to be passed on to my daughter, as my sons cannot wear this woman's crest. (They can use the other thirteen crests that our family owns).

When I tell my stories I use my robe. I bring my drum, given to me by my uncle, T. Richard Baker. And sometimes, I bring special silk screened prints my dear friend Desmond Bowker gave me to illustrate my stories. One day I will wear a cedar hat. When I am done my presentations I sing a song that says, "I'll see you again." We do not have a word for good bye in our language. We always say, "I'll see you again."

My mother told me about a relative who did talk not very nice about my performances. My mother honoured me by her words when she said, "You have a gift. This wasn't something you learned. It was given to you. And you can't help but share this gift." She was referring to my singing and storytelling. I am very moved by these words as they really are true. I did not learn this as I grew up on *Haida Gwaii*. I learned it later as I was living in a city. This city I lived in felt so big. I felt so alone. Like I was the only Haida person living there. I wanted to connect to my culture in some way and this was the only way I knew how.

I perform to instill pride in my children. This is pride I did not have as I grew up. This is not my parents' fault, but society's fault. The shame continued until I became an adult. My Raven children are proud of themselves. And I will continue to perform until they bring my grandchildren and great-grandchildren up on stage with me.

TRACEY LINDBERG

DANCING BY YOURSELF

Deanna Lawrence hates me. It's true. My friend Jackie told me. Deanna and I went to high school together. She was part of that crowd that everyone hates. Too much make-up, too much anger, too little conscience. I cowered from those girls. I was afraid they would notice my skin was too brown. I was scared they would notice my mother was not the same as their mothers. I would pretend to be the same. I would laugh the same way all annoying high school girls do (lots of teeth —we're so happy!); I would socialize the way they do (dating the token pimply-faced hockey player); and I would defer to their greatness.

I was miserable.

I moved away from my high school town one week after high school. I had one plan in mind: get away.

I moved to a city in Northern Saskatchewan. I got a job at an A&W serving greasy hamburgers and cheerless smiles to people living in a seedy section of town. Seedy in Saskatchewan means a neighbourhood with a high Indian population. When I worked the night shift I would bundle up at 2:00 and walk the mile through icy winds and streets to the duplex I shared with my mother.

People at work told me I should not expose myself to such danger. I lived in a "dangerous" neighbourhood and was supposed to watch out for myself. I guess this meant that the mostly Indian street I lived on had a high crime rate. Violent crime was very high there. I was never afraid of it, though. I guess I supposed that my light brown skin and the white features I inherited from my father would protect me from white violence. I also believed that my dark hair, high cheekbones and black eyes would allow me to fade into the Indian world. I believed myself to be a cultural chameleon.

As I poured the root beer and wiped down all that could be wiped down at the drive-in one day a man approached me and asked me if there were any good bars near by. I pointed to the National Hotel across the road and told him a lot of our customers went there. He looked at me disapprovingly and told me it was a little "dark" there for his taste. I told him I had no idea what he was talking about.

But I did. I knew exactly what he was talking about. When I was in Grade Three my teacher broached an impromptu discussion about freckles and skin tone. I can't remember the context. What I can remember is sitting there expectantly as she walked through the classroom, pupil by pupil, examining us for freckles. When she reached my desk, she placed her hard-working liver spotted hand under my chin and pronounced, "you're too dark, I can't see any."

And went on.

I was so scared and humiliated. I was afraid everyone in the all-white classroom knew that I was too dark. To be too dark made you suspect. Suspect made you Indian. Indian made you different. Different made you an outsider.

This fear of being different sat on my desk through junior high school. Every time we walked into history class that fear shifted to my stomach and made me feel nauseous. Much to my relief, we never discussed Indians while we learned about the history of Canada. Not the Indians I knew, anyway. We talked about savages and morally bankrupt heathens who refused to get out of the way of colonists and modernists.

These people were so unlike my aunts and uncles who laughed, cried and danced their way through the weddings and funerals I attended in Grande Prairie. My mom told me she was never going back there. I think being a Belcourt in Alberta was a really hard thing for her. More bad blood in those bar rooms than there was beer. She's surprised when I tell her that want to practice law there. I think that I am more proud of being Indian than she was allowed to be. I have the security that a Masters Law degree from Harvard can insulate you with. I guess that's part of it. I want to be the first Indian practitioner there. I want those people—the ones who told my mother that the dress she borrowed from a neighbour to go to a school dance looked too old on her—that my mother has done some amazing things. I am an extension of her beauty and her wisdom.

Deanna Lawrence knows none of this. All she knows is that by the time I reached University I was Indian. I am so proud of that. I am proud of knowing I am one of the fibres in a beautifully woven blanket of peoplehood. I am strong and giving and intertwined with the fibres of thousands of others who have shed tears, blood and fears and finally "come out" as Indians. Deanna Lawrence can never know that I have heard my mother called a squaw, been called a wagon-burner by my sister's first boyfriend. Deanna Lawrence can never understand the horror of being called a squaw in front of one hundred high school students while giving them a lecture on summer job search techniques.

When I was in my last year of my Arts Degree I was arrested for chaining myself to Indian Affairs. I was part of a radicalised group of Indian youth protesting Indian Affairs funding cut-backs. This was not about me, that's something Deanna Lawrence can't know. This was about my grandfather who couldn't legally vote in Canada until he was forty. This was about my sixteen year old mother giving birth to my sister one year after leaving her mother's home and shedding her role as the principal caregiver to her younger siblings.

When I got into law school I thought I had left Deanna Lawrence behind. Not so. One of the most open and beautifully honest people I met was Jenny Melin. One problem—Jenny Melin lived with Deanna. Jenny was cold and indifferent to me at first. After a year or so we opened up to each other to the point where I could ask her why she was so estranged from me initially. She told me Deanna hated me and that she had convinced Jackie that I was a liar. I knew what she meant. I was a liar because the fact that I 'came to be' Indian had not come out until I came to University.

Deanna Lawrence wanders in and out of my life. She is there listening when I lecture about Indian law and government. She is a silent but hanging judge holding court over all that is brown. I let her into the room too often. She sits with me as I watch *Pow Wow Highway*, *Dances With Wolves*, and *Black Robe*. She dances over my shoulder while I round dance. She stands silently while I pray to the Creator. But I know she's there.

She waits for my mistake, a chink in my armour to reveal who I really am. I admire her patience. She's seen me the whole time, an unwilling observer to this transition I have to make. She is not an impartial observer. She's an errant scientist recording only the data that reinforce her theory.

And now I am at Harvard Law School. This is hard. There are five other Indians in the population of the student body. Only one of them I have met is "out." She relishes Indianhood and wears it like a head dress. She can bond with me because we are both brown. That is all, and that is everything. As I sit in Race Relations (an eighty hour class) during one of the two hours devoted to the founder of this and every nation I wonder if I can speak. Deanna Lawrence sits beside me and reminds me I have never lived on a reserve. Surely, I admonish her, it's relevant that my family is Indian. Also, I tell her from the side of my mouth, in a modern world Indians can come from all backgrounds, especially urban ones.

Deanna snickers and I sit there in silence, cringing occasionally at the racial stereotypes an innocent black man is making at the front of the class.

I met another Cree woman on a street corner in Harvard Square once. She wore the colours of her nation on her jacket and I approached her immediately. How surprised she must have been at my clinging words and demeanor towards her. She told me that she was thinking of applying here. Don't do it, I whispered, Deanna Lawrence is here. She's waiting to take all that matters through anthropologist eyes and re-create it.

Since I have been in Cambridge, I have been asked:
1. If one of my parents was white;
2. If I knew that I didn't look Indian;
3. If I have lived on a reserve;
4. If I felt 'at one' with the earth;
5. If alcoholism was a big problem for my people;
6. If I worried that I would never marry an Indian man as I am so obviously above any intellectual attainment they could reach;
7. Why my last name was so obviously European.

In addition, many people have expressed surprise that my mother currently lives on a reserve, that I have brothers who do not associate culturally with Indian people, and that I sift all of the information that I receive through a filter of race. Like Deanna, they need to know the basis of my identity and whether I am really Indian. I choose not to silence debate so I answer each question honestly and thoughtfully. Still, I am constantly offended and angry at this imposition, no, at this inquisition, because I don't think every member of the class is subjected to this intense racial and historical scrutiny.

The white man I care about most here told me he thought I looked Indian. These two facts are not arbitrarily related. He made room for me in his theory of Indianness. He had never met an Indian before. I have become the standard that he assesses Indian issues by. It is onerous and misplaced, but I relish that responsibility. He lets me tell him, not answer him, about issues I think are important. He has never heard of Deanna Lawrence and I am so afraid he will meet her.

"*Awasis*. Child"
"*Awasees*. Child."
"*Napew*. Man."
"*Napew*. Man."

"*Iskwew*. Woman."

Sitting up higher at the desk, "*Iskwew*. Woman."

I love that word. It is strong. It is powerful. It has been denigrated, altered, brutalized, and we still are *iskwew*. Not squaw. Not men. Women. *Iskwewak*.

I want Deanna Lawrence and those that ask too much, speak too painful words to understand this. I was born with brown eyes. I see *iskwewak* everywhere in this world of mine. I see us in the leaves dancing multicoloured and exotically grinding wildly through the streets. I see us in the black and brown earth; permanent and changeable, elemental and pure. I observe us in the swish swishing of brown black and sometimes blonde braids swinging left and right across shoulders, backs, and buttocks. Sometimes when I go to the mall I think that I see us coming towards me. A girlfriend told me once that she can tell who the other lesbians are in a room. I guess I can do that too. If there is an Indian woman in the room I know she's there. It's something in the way that we look at each other. It's a look full of meaning and devoid of meaning. You can't know it and I won't share it with you. And yet Deanna Lawrence wants me to tell her why I see this.

She probably couldn't know that I have a little difficulty with spotting Indian men. I sometimes feel like they have all deserted me, deserted me in their search for blonde white women and their cars. They must have cars or they really would not be dating up, would they? I get quite mad at Indian men sometimes. I know they have a fight to fight too, I just wish they would stand next to me and fight it sometimes. It's hard enough standing there alone with Deanna over my shoulder, I can't bear the thought of them standing beside her.

There's little danger of that. Once when I was in my undergrad, Deanna Lawrence and I had a chance meeting at a mall in Saskatoon. A mutual friend of ours suggested that we go for coffee. I wanted to go to the mall food fair. Deanna said to us, somewhat reproachfully, that it was just another place for Indians to hang out. There is so much hate wrapped up in that I was unable to untie it. My hands were bound and my mouth was gagged. I am mad at myself to this day for not saying something.

Something about the Indian woman. The Indian woman, now she is the one I can see best. She glows in the dark to me. She can wear her pride like a pair of indiscreet underwear, like a muffler or like a jacket. Her pain is less obvious. It is in winces, grimaces, and twinges of unease. I see it because I feel it. It's like being a stranger in a crowd of good friends, this upheaval to city life. I should have told Deanna that I can spot that woman at twenty feet and I will give her no personal space when I find her.

And although being with Deanna leaves me senseless I can smell the Indian woman. Cigarette and tea breath. Moosehide and Oscar de la Renta. She can hide it, but I'd know that smell anywhere: woman and wild, *iskwew* and life—it's all around us but only I can smell it here.

My white girlfriends are patient with me. "Maybe it's a brain tumour," they must think when I tell them for the third time in one day that I can smell sweetgrass, rich and pungent, as it wafts in past the smog and grime to my nose in the Yellow Cab. I have never told Deanna about the smell.

How could she understand that? She would not find it amusing that I know that she has no smell. I would be insulting her and she would not know it. I hate to say it because I know it's race biased, but they all smell the same. Sure it's Anne Klein, Perry Ellis, Versace, whoever, but it's the same white guy smell that they have bottled and bought and besotted themselves with.

I smell gamey smells and smoky wildness, and the nostril caressing flavour of tanned hide in Deanna's absence.

When I am at McDonald's, Burger King, any place—I imagine I am eating dried meat, moose meat, deer sausage, anything from a place where the animals choose to give their earthbodies for my sustenance. I wonder vaguely if I should invite her for dinner.

We could watch television after dinner. Even that is not safe. I look for the Indian there too. Mostly when I find her here she is a hollow image of whom I know her to be. She is fat, she has long unkempt hair. She is quite often drunk and disorderly. It makes me long for the racist ideologies of the seventies that had us all looking fuckable and feelable. No virtue—only lusty looking tasting dark skinned white women.

Here in Cambridge I never get to meet the Indian woman. Last week I gave a speech to a room full of polite listeners. I tried to express to them, respectfully and kindly, that I am angry. I am angry because I have to be there. Angry because I am teaching them. Angry because they can't hear me. I see them listen and the room is silent so I know they are listening. They just can't hear me. The one person who I think can hear me is, of course, Indian. He gives me a beautiful gift of forum and silence and I know he's there and I know he's listening. He puts me in touch with several other Indian women. It's an early Christmas gift that I am too overwhelmed by. Yet I hear Deanna's voice, a shrill echo, and I cannot speak my words any longer.

I realize now that I am angry at how she shuts down my senses. Imposing on me a code of conduct and a pattern of behaviour. I am speechless because she disregards my statements. I am not being true to myself, she tells all who will hear her. I am denying my history, I know she imagines. And I let her in.

I let her in every time I make observations based on a past she disdainfully ignores. This past, this collective history, includes images and understandings I refuse to shut out. I have seen women adored and word caressed. I have seen our women imprisoned and beaten. I have smelled pain so acute that it makes my eyes water. I have tasted joy that ecstacizes my mouth. I refuse to share any of these sensations with Deanna. It took me a long time to collect them and own them. I will pass them on to life with more sensitive ears, eyes, noses, mouths and fingertips.

Ssssh, I will tell them. You don't have to fear the Aryans and the KKK, you can smell their hatred and feel their fear. It's the devil you know that you should watch out for.

And I do watch her. I listen for her: the heavy shuffle of a far away presence being left behind as I reclaim all that my grandmothers and grandfathers left for me. I can hear them now because I no longer let Deanna Lawrence drown them out.

Laura A. Marsden

Cedar, Thunderbird and the Bear:
Graduation of the Thunderbird

You could hear the crackling of the burning cedar from the shell. Looking to the West, Thunderbird decided he wanted to attend a ceremony of the people. He had been thinking of this for ages. There was so much to consider, the size of the doorway, the reception of the people and the reason why. He began planning by remembering the history and his beginning. It was just about the same time as the Earth was formed. He had left the planet of his birth, his parents, his grandparents and his childhood. He remembered being young and fluffy and awkward as he began to walk the Earth. His ancestors never left him because they could reach across the universe and touch each other wingtip to wingtip. We must have been prehistoric he imagined. He remembers, having the ability to enhance the spiritual journey of the human beings according to each their age. He could never be older or younger than someone in order to create the best environment for learning. This was a special skill and only life's experience could be the teacher.

As a youth, of course, he was the kind that had difficulty in balancing himself. The Wind especially could blow him this way and that quite easily. He remembers when he was very young, about a month old, he had fallen from somewhere on to a soft mossy surface. Looking up, the Little Baby Thunderbird saw his first beautiful young woman. She could smile so sweet it made him fall over in his nest. He soon fell asleep and asked the girl's mother to remember him. The following day the girl's special name became Little Baby Thunderbird. This naming confirmed his existence and allowed him to go forward with his life.

It was some time later, about teen age, when Baby grew up. He had been flying for some time now and still hadn't realized his purpose in life. Little Thunderbird was lonely, so lonely his tears would make a lake falling on the Earth. He just wanted to be young again and walk on the Earth once more. In stubbornesss he started to research everywhere and observe the little people on this planet they call Earth. He remembered the lakes and he felt responsible. He would peck around the Longhouse which was like a little matchbox and wondered how he could open the doorway. There were all kinds of lights coming from inside, little alluring sparkles of light. All of a sudden, there was a great explosion and Thunderbird was hurled back fifty million miles into the air. What was that feeling? Don't they know how powerful I am, what I could do to them with one footstep? So Thunderbird spent another million years draped in the sky and was enforced to portray a perfect image of serenity.

After another million years, Thunderbird became fitful and bored with life. One night after many sleepless nights he decided he would research his dilemma. He discovered there was one animal that was most similar to mankind, one that had a nature similar to his except he couldn't fly. It was the Bear. It was the Spirit of the Bear that had scared him away, the protector of Mother Earth and Brother of Man. Bear had lived among the prickly cedar trees since the beginning of time. Bear told the story of how the Cedar Medicine filled little pockets of air around the Earth and was very cleansing. He remembered Thunderbird when he had just about toppled the Longhouse years ago. It was the Bear who had given him permission to enter the Longhouse. The people had felt sorry for Thunderbird but thought maybe they had taken on too great a challenge. It wasn't until years later that Thunderbird realized the turning point and purpose of his life began with a stepped on cedar branch, the fear of facing the Bear and his beating heart.

Out of curiosity, loneliness and fear, Thunderbird was welcomed into a world which was alien to him. He had to win the heart of the Bear and develop the Age of Reason. Thunderbird has gained many friends. He grew to understand the needs of the people and Mother Earth. Thunderbird sits in the sky and is protector and visionary for the trees, the birds, the animals and the two legged. Through serious research and education you can see him hovering over the night sky. Yet, watch carefully because he's the hardest to see when he is beyond vision and beyond reason. He is mystical and magical and powerful. He loves all living things because he discovered the doorway to his heart at the Longhouse, past the cedar trees, past the Bear and back to the pathways of the universe.

GRAHAM SCOTT PROULX

THE CREATIVE LINK TO THE SPIRIT

Countless masterful works of art and literature have graced humankind over the millennia. Movements come and go and the ideas and theories that define good art and literature have changed along with them. One of the constant elements is the creative seed within the artist. All great works began as an inkling in the artists imagination. Only the practised stroke of a brush and blending of paint of a master, can truly translate that spark into the light of day. An idea may be born from inspiration, or it may be realized through inspiration, or the two may work together, nurturing one another. Either way, both the idea and the inspiration that inevitably accompanies it, come from a mysterious, intangible source—the realm of the spirit.

Many proponents of psychological thought would argue against this. They believe the source of creativity to be a part of the internal psyche. The subconscious, instead of the Spirit, directs the consciousness of the artist. I prefer a less psycho-analytical approach. For me, psychology only serves to addle the issue; it removes the spiritual element from its subject, objectively breaking the whole into the sum in a cold, unfeeling manner. As an artist and a writer, I am unable at this time in my career to stand away objectively. At times, I am so overwhelmed by inspiration that I become frantic and fear bringing the seed into this world; to translate the inner vision into something visually concrete. The feelings I experience at these moments do not stem from my unconscious, which implies that they come to me in my head. Instead, they originate in my midriff, where my spirit dwells. My head only serves as a kind of translator and embellisher. The insubstantial swelling of pure ecstasy in my belly is so real and so potent, that the only feasible explanation is a spiritual phenomenon.

The very word 'inspiration' comes from the Latin words for 'spirit' and 'inhale'. A breath of spirit. Not unlike taking a sniff of one's favourite flower and wondering at the pure sense of peace and calm the fragrance infuses in us, my spirit too draws on such wonders for inspiration. My fail-safe source for inspiration and ideas comes from Mother Earth herself. Breathtaking landscapes and the enthralling myriad of macroscopic details in our natural surroundings all lend themselves to my work.

Other artists are similarity affected by Mother Earth. Some, like Vincent Van Gogh, are vigorously stimulated on an emotional level: "Is it not emotion, the sincerity of one's feelings for nature, that drives us? And if the emotions are sometimes so strong that one works without knowing one works, when sometimes the strokes come with a continuity and a coherence like words in a speech or a letter..."[1] By emulating the emotions that he saw plainly in the bright sun washed landscapes of Southern France, Van Gogh transcribed onto canvas through his unique style of expression, moving portraits of nature.

The creative seeds that gave Van Gogh his emotional release exists in us all. To what degree the individual nurtures these seeds is a matter of choice and confidence. I had very little confidence in my artistic abilities before studying at the En'owkin International School of Creative Writing and Visual Arts. But thanks to the guidance, encouragement and constructive criticism from my mentors and peers, I now have the confidence to explore the mediums of my choosing.

Like myself, Daphne Odjig, Anishnaabe painter extraordinaire, lacked the intestinal fortitude in her early years to let the seeds come to full blossom, but always saw herself as a painter. It was not until she beheld the works of master painters in The Louvre that she was truly inspired to leave over to the guiding hand of her spirit: "I wished I had the courage to put into painting as those people did... but do I have the courage?"[2] The emotions and passion that the masters of the past breathed into their works was enough to set her own spirit soaring and set her style apart from the rest.

Emily Carr experienced similar feelings when she beheld the original works of the Impressionists and Post-Impressionists in Paris; "... after months of careful deliberation and comparison that I found in the new work that which I had long been seeking for... Contrary to my having 'given up inspiration' I have only just found it and I could not go back to the old dead way of working after I've tasted the joys of the new..."[3] Here, Emily Carr has clearly been moved by the masterful works of others and in harnessing the ensuing flows of inspiration, she embarked on the most prolific and ground-breaking stage of her career.

The struggle that the artist undergoes, myself included, to bring the inspired vision to life is articulated succinctly by graphic artist M.C. Escher. He describes his creative process as a two-fold endeavour:

"The process begins with the search for a visual form such as will interpret as clearly as possible one's train of thought. Usually a long time elapses before I decide that I have got it clear in my mind. Yet a mental image is something completely different from a visual image, and however one exerts oneself, one can never manage to capture the fullness of that perfection which hovers in the mind and which one thinks of, quite falsely, as something that is 'seen'. After a long series of attempts I manage to cast my lovely dream into the defective visual mould of a detailed conceptual sketch. After this, to my great relief, there dawns the second phase, that is the making of the graphic print, for now the spirit can take its rest while the work is taken over by the hands."[4]

Escher was thus quoted when he was already an established artist. The confidence and skill mastery were already his. But as he states, and I concur, there is only so much left to the mind. The source of the artistic vision is by far the larger contributor. The 'divinely inspired' works of the spirit is expressed. The energy passed on by Creator or God or Who Have You is translated vividly or subtly into works that profoundly affect the beholder. The mental image provided by the Spirit and fuelled by inspiration becomes a reality and another masterpiece is born.

Notes:

1) Wallace, Robert, <u>The World of Van Gogh</u>: Time-Life Books, New York, 1974, (p. 91).

2) Vanderburgh, R.M. & Southcott, M.E., <u>A Paintbrush In My Hand-Daphne Odjig</u>: National Heritage/National History Inc., Toronto, Ontario, 1992, (p. 87).

3) Shadbolt, Doris, <u>Emily Carr</u>; J.J. Douglas Ltd., North Vancouver, BC, 1975, (p. 12).

4) Brigham, John E., (trans.), <u>The Graphic Work of M.C. Escher</u>: Hawthorn Books, Inc., Publishers, New york, 1960, (pp. 7-8).

SHARRON PROULX-TURNER

healing and dis-ease:
    a return to mother
       to creation
          to movement

"blood rushes to my fingers and the frozen blankets off the line"

they say it's hard to talk about death
sometimes it's hard to talk about life
death's a new beginning

my mother isn't good to me when she's alive
she doesn't like me

right from the start she doesn't like me
she says I tried to kill her from in her womb
tells anyone who'll listen

I'm the biggest born
a fat baby

goat's milk bread and sugar's how I stay that way
too slow for cow's milk is what they say
soft in the head

I'm the slowest to walk
the slowest to talk

I'm toilet trained very young
and then begin to dirty my drawers again
so I'm put back on the diapers

I wear a diaper and suck a soother til I'm in school
I'm beaten a lot and raped by many men and women
and that's not just the half of it

my mother destroys my childhood pictures as they come along
some say I make that up and rip them up myself

it's not true though
so I never see a picture of that fat baby
or the cross-eyed girl with crooked teeth

they are close my family
thing is the closeness is unhealthy

keeps the cocoon brilliant with its own poison
my family touches wrong
there's no telling who'll blackout and go hogwild

there's one thing about my family though
never a dull moment

sharp knives maybe
but never a dull moment

because I see my family that way
as a mass of bone and fibre and light
for my kids' and their kids' kids

I stop the drinking

the violence
the incest

not that I stop going there every sunday like a sun dial
when my mother is alive

I cook
I clean
take care of the kids

and make sure the breakables are out of the way of the adults
thing is I'm not no saint you understand

no angel either
but by golly gee holy smokes I'm workin on stuff
and that there's one weird family I come from

my mother phones me twice in my adult life
the second time she calls she can't stop choking

she quits smoking about six years or so before
that's about the same time she switches
from beer to rum and coke

drinks to blackouts
she's at work when she calls

she's crying and sounds scared and scary at the same time
I go and pick her up and take her to her doctor
this is a friday
sunday she has emergency surgery
they're going to remove her left lung

they close her up after they open her
and there's nothing there but cancer

she's very ill from then on
dies eight months later

two days before my mother calls me up and choking
I call her up to tell her today I'm leaving my husband
so while my mother's dying I'm feeling

pretty good
and I feel guilty and ashamed
and happier than I ever felt in my life

not that I wish death on my mother
but the knowing is so delicious
so liberating

I can see her dying every day
after a few months

she wants me to go to her house
and clean every second day
which I do

she wants me with her when she goes to kemo
she wants me to help her pick out scarves to cover her baldness

she wants me to get her tea
she wants me to feed her
she wants me to soothe and swab the open sores inside her mouth

she wants me to sing to her

she wants me to massage her when she

smells of cancer and morphine and death
and her bones are her only curves

and then her bones get the cancer too
too painful to the touch
and then her brain

and then her brain forgets to tell her body what to do
forgets to tell her body how to take her into death

any day now
the hospital folks say
any day now

day after day after day after day
I love my mother

for a long time after her death I'm sick with hurt
and glee and anger and grief
not any more though

then this summer my mother comes to me in a dream
she tells me she is different

she can help me now she says
she can come to me like my grandmothers
I am not too comfortable with this

so I frame a photo of my mom when she is just a girl
a picture at her first foster home

behind her left lung there's laundry on the line
abuse and fear and danger that's just hangin' out to dry

I don't believe for one minute that all that's written comes from a sacred place. yet, for me as a métis woman, it's imperative to be respectful of the sacredness of this gift, this ability to write. I know how all-important my respect and acknowledgment of the great spirit is to the process of writing. I am a vehicle for this particular kind of beauty and knowledge and healing. the more I'm aware of this, the more I put my faith in this, the more powerful my writing becomes. writing creates a knowing inside beauty. the beauty is felt from the words for the reader. for the writer, the beauty is between the spirit world and the word. the reader senses and feels the beauty because the spirit world exists inside, within what's being told. and the spirit world comes alive through voice.

in 1986 my mother died. since 1986, twelve years now, I have single-parented two children into young adulthood, presented my two-spirit self, completed a bachelor's and master's degree in english, written three books, facilitated more than one hundred anti-racism and homophobia workshops, recovered memories and aftershock of extreme violence and ritual abuse during my childhood, openly embraced my métis identity, which shamed my mother so overwhelmingly during her short life. my mother's body was eaten by cancer. some elders say when we are unable to heal from past traumas, the pain turns inward to become disease. this is not to say people are somehow to blame for their own illnesses or that those who are able to heal from past traumas will escape disease; rather, this is a paradox.

after my mother's death, my life opened up in ways I hadn't imagined. now I could freely and publicly and openly assert myself as a métis woman. I was now free to mingle in my own communities, without the constant watchful, disapproving eye and sharp tongue of my mother. I wanted to do something for my mother and my grandmother, for my children, so I went to university to please my ancestors and benefit those not yet born. I found new communities, aboriginal people and people of colour who were like-minded and articulate on matters of race and class in ways I hadn't imagined.

I grew up during a time of consciousness raising, AIM and civil rights. I didn't know much about universities except that my grandmother and my mother said education was the key to a better life for the future generations and encouraged me to go. my grandmother gave me a dictionary for my fourth birthday. she'd look in there and she'd see a word and she'd tell a story long as your arm. for years I thought that dictionary was a story book. my grandmother was a métis two spirit woman whose children, my mother and her sisters and brothers, were taken by the government and raised as farm slaves in white foster care.

I was born into racism and homophobia and poverty, into incest, into alcoholism and shame, ritual abuse and severe violence. for those who may not know, in the words of shirley turcotte, herself a métis woman and survivor of ritual abuse:

> ritual abuse is the breaking down of a person—for example, sexually and mentally—by an organized or semi-organized group in a repetitive fashion over time. this abuse can be perpetrated within a range of institutional settings, including religious settings, residential schools, business settings, hospitals, the military, penal systems or community-based settings, just to name a few.

and in the words of catherine gould, a middle class white psychologist who treats children with post-trauma stress:

> ritual abuse is a brutal form of abuse in which the victim is assaulted at every conceivable level, usually by multiple perpetrators of both sexes, over an extended period of time. the physical abuse is so severe that it often involves torture and killing. the sexual abuse is typically sadistic, painful, and humiliating. the psychological abuse relies upon terrorization of the victim, mind-altering drugs, and mind-control techniques. the spiritual abuse causes victims to feel that they are utterly worthless.

to put it mildly, I have suffered atrocities beyond many people's imaginings. I have learned to appreciate life, to appreciate my body, to appreciate my voice, to appreciate honesty, in a way that's not expressible in words. I guess this shows in my appearance now. I am happy.

this is my first time being invited to sit on a panel at this university. I attended the university of calgary and graduated in 1994. my mentors here were pamela mccallum, a white middle class english prof who taught me the value of my own intelligence and critical abilities, the late chuck steele, a white english prof who came from poverty, whose presence in my life was a gift, the late kathleen martindale, a white women's studies prof who also came from poverty, who showed unwavering faith in my skills as an educator, and aritha van herk and fred wah—aritha van herk, a white middle class creative writing prof whose bold red ink on my very first english essay read, "this is no essay, but you sure as hell can write," and fred wah, a mixed race chinese-canadian creative writing prof who opened a rich and powerful path in my world, my present path as a writer. and one woman, aruna srivastava, a mixed race south asian english prof who has become a dear friend, offered compassion and constant support throughout a difficult and unexpected turn of events which continues to contribute to a disease, a fundamental disempowerment of me as a person to this day.

though I am indeed happy, I have changed. I am not the woman I was. not even close. turned inward and there's an intrinsic spunk, an energy, a passion, that's gone missing. and I've wondered, what can I do? how to get back what was stolen from me?

during my university days I continued the human rights activist work I'd been doing since the late 60s. I was among the women who contributed to the opening of a women's centre on campus. I facilitated workshops on racism and classism and sexism and homophobia and pointed out all the white, heterosexual faces in the grad classes. I was born white skinned to a brown skinned mother, and I know how much privilege whiteness brings with it. I became known as a discrete and sensitive person who knew of the student services on campus and I had countless women approach me for help and support over the years. consequently, I got to know a lot more than one woman perhaps ought to know about which profs in which departments were practising racists, misogynists, homophobes, and even rapists. some of these issues were brought to the attention of administrative people at this university and I was invited to attend a series of meetings. things were progressing; then, the process ended abruptly. I was given a 'choice' to either sign a memo saying I would concentrate on my thesis and stop all political work on campus or be charged with misconduct by a dean for allegedly spreading false rumours about a prof. subsequent to this, my thesis, an autobiographical account of a part of my childhood, was delayed by a year while it was scrutinized by a university lawyer. subsequent to this, my thesis was 'sealed,' which means my thesis was not published by the university because of concerns about lawsuits. my thesis appears in no one's office, in no library. my extensive research on ritual abuse and my personal story are literally locked up in a vault. and a version of my thesis, published under a pseudonym in 1995, though available in several university libraries across canada and the states, is not in the holdings at my home library, even after requests. subsequent to all of this, many women, faculty who called themselves 'feminists,' said I was a traitor to all feminists and to this day won't meet my eyes. and since then, my academic mentors who are living and/or who are white do not meet my eyes.

this story has many gaps, gaps which I am not able to fill. inside these gaps is my dis-ease, my disempowerment. I've told this story to a respected Elder in my community, an Elder who has three degrees from universities in alberta. he said two things: first, he said their university system still models themselves after the 'crown,' where they cling to their 15th century notion of manifest destiny and the superiority of white upper class European boys who are left motherless at an early age because they are raised in boarding schools. their system is a disease, a cancer that's eating away at them. then he said, take a vacation.

Janet Rogers

Cowichan Hills: A Hunting Experience

Salish hunter took me high on a mountain top to see what he could hunt down. A younger Salish man joined us, eager to become hunter. We arrived in the hills at midnight. A full bright moon seemed even fuller and brighter from the tip top place we inhabited. But even Grandmother Moon could not reveal the vast landscape below us. We waited until morning light for that view. There we were, hunter, young man and me, tenting it on a rock. The hunter fed me midnight secrets to draw me near. He growled his power, and I welcomed him to me. We were not prepared for the crisp cold that kept us from sleep. We shivered together in the nylon dome, missing out on nocturnal emissions, inspired by the site. I was breaking all the rules by being there. They were both healing and I was bleeding and needless to say the Gods did not approve.

I woke up alone, groggy and cold with red stained thighs. The hunters were gone to capture their prize, while my gifts were delivered just outside the tent flap. The beginning of the day held cool, clear mountain air laced with cedar and frost. I filled both my lungs and head with this powerful elixir. "Thank you" I didn't forget. Fully emerged from the tent, the second gift was soon to be realized. A carpet of green hidden by night's wrapping filled my view, in every hue, everywhere. I was on top of the world. I discovered, seeing with God's eyes, a surreal landscape dream. The trees held tight, making a tug of war with the mist before it was burned away from the clouded terrace. The fog performed a slow striptease revealing more of the wonderment below to my anxious eyes and swelling heart. This was the BC I was introduced to years ago. It was comforting to know she still resides here.

I broke away from the visual meditation to tend to cooling coals and rebuild heat.

Though there was not another body in sight, I did not feel alone. Nor did the natural silence unnerve me. After a cup of familiar coffee, I warmed up with a walk along the crunchy path once used to carry away freshly cut logs to market. These hills made me high. The strength and energy of the rock below instructed me to walk lightly with respect, to stay mindful with every step. I walked onward, taking in new perspectives of the spiky textured still life below. The altitude, and lack of sleep winded me. The sun was full out now. I found a setting of mossy rocks where I climbed about like a student let out for recess. I quickly became familiar with the grooves and handles for safe play. A flat topped rock made for a solid bed, where I layed down inviting the warmth of the sun to blanket me. There I drifted ever so slightly into sleep. My head fell onto a mossy pillow, and there I mentally repeated "Thank you for this day, thank you for this day."

BANG! A distant blast roused me out of the light slumber. Silence—wonder. BANG! Again. Exciting hunting sounds come from below. I rose off the fuzzy rock to make my way back on the fully lit trail to camp. On the way, I fantasized about a limp deer body carried on the hunter's strong back, slumped onto the ground ready for the gutting knife. I would take part by picture taking. Snapping up the liquid red, the strings of flesh, the removal of innards onto the stony ground. Yet no one is at camp, so I climbed to the top of the truck to increase my gaze. Trees and nothing but trees met my visual search. I rested on my back on the metal platform, facing the sky and was drawn in by small puffs of hyper white clouds which grew, and blossomed, like solid bubbles, then floated away. I am amused by this entertainment for what seemed like hours. White billowy beauty, growing like organisms to outrageous sizes before my eyes.

When the hunters returned, they were hungry. I learned the blasts were target practice. Itchy fingers anxious to work the gun. They brought back only their appetites. The young one made a sloppy sandwich and devoured it, half conscious of the act. He picked up his rifle and wondered off, down the trail. The Salish hunter stood on a high rock looking over the cedar greens. He feeds on air, and sunshine and is content as a King in his Kingdom. I snapped his picture, and pointed out the natural cabaret of exploding cloud shapes above us. He is delighted with this finding, so we stand in silence and watch. He told me he noticed a small pond along the trail where we can wash up. We boarded the truck to get there. He stripped, I felt shy. He told me to speak to the water, to ask it to cleanse me. He waded in, pulling up handfuls of cool liquid onto his skin. I kept my rubber boots and bra on and approached carefully. I cleansed my legs first, then my face and hair. I didn't feel beautiful, but I feel cleansed. Without towels to dry, we stumbled back onto the road then back to camp. We waited for the young one to return and in the meantime, we packed things, ready to move camp.

We took a slow, motorized tour to another side. Upon arriving at the new location, the hunters looked to me and said "you commin" in an invitational manner. As we headed into the trees, I slung my camera crossways on my chest. "How do you do this" I enquired my armed guides. "Just stay close." Our steps slowed and quieted the deeper we entered the woods. The young one broke away, taking a separate path. We continued to walk long steps, taking care to place our feet onto clear ground so as not to make snapping sounds with twigs. With arms bent, and slightly raised, we tip-toed and balanced our way along an unbroken path. I felt I was dancing. A light footed, slow choreographed combination of twists and bends. No words were passed, only thoughts communicated by looks. The tension was exciting and sensual. The dance continued. A human whistle sounded, revealing the position of the young hunter. We approached a set of clumpy bushes and were startled by a rushing sound of frightened flight. We froze! Hearts pounding loudly! The hunter aimed! A grouse took to the air. The hunter and I shared a relieved smile. We journeyed on to the other side of the woods meeting up with our third party to recap the failed attempt.

The rest of the day was spent moving to different locations, sometimes travelling higher and farther up the green mountain, performing the same step/dance in quiet hopefulness. Walking in a circle, always coming back to the beginning. By evening another strategy was being formed. We had stopped in a clearing and ate potatoes cooked black in their skins. I offered the hunters fresh coffee as a stimulant for the hunt. The fresh air and lack of sleep wearied me, so I made the back seat my bed for the night. Doubled sleeping bags were my ally against the cold dark dampness. The hunters prepared to begin "pit-lamping" while taking my sleeping body along for the ride. They fussed over dead batteries in a bright spot light, meant to flush out deer at a distance by it's glare.

All throughout the night, they drove at a snail's pace along gravel paths, invading the sleeping woods with light. The gentle rocking of the truck churned my blood and lulled me into a beautiful doze. By morning, I realized we were parked in the same spot from where we began at sunset. Again, travelling in a circle. The hunters settled in for the big sleep. Peace was all around us like a natural blanket. In a place like that, it's easy to feel God's watchful eyes upon you. Safe and unnerving at the same time. Hunter's eyes closed to the sun coming up to put an end to another day of work.

The last day of the hunt had begun with a groggy lightness. The excited hopefulness was now fading into a quiet acceptance of defeat. Visions of a lifeless carcass strapped to the roof of the truck bleeding it's last blood drops, were fading too. We moved forward into the day playfully. We continued to drive up high ridges and descend into valleys where families fished the lakes. The boys parked halfway between heaven and earth, to take off on untrodden paths. I stayed behind, in the limbo place, and drifted off into a magical dreamland, a healing rest. They returned just as my eyes re-opened, suggesting a synchronisation of our systems. They presented me with large abstract shaped fungus gifts which they asked me to paint for them. We celebrated this find with grilled cheese sandwiches. We ate heartily enjoying the perks of the natural diner around us. We spied a grouse walking casually along the road, as we packed ourselves back into the truck. The hunter took aim, I took cover. Then came the BLAST, and there lay the limp feathered body. I had the hunter pose for a picture with his kill, as a half tribute, half joke to our hunting adventure. Hunters do look handsome in their trophy pictures. Perhaps that's because they always pose beside something dead and that comparison can only be advantageous to them.

Knowing still, the deer would stay out of sight, we journeyed along more roads, new roads, looking hard into the woods from our mobile vantage point. We crawled by the truck to the end of a path and back again. It had begun to drizzle which gave the hunter new hope. But at last he relented and carried ourselves and our belongings back out onto the highway that would lead us home. Once there, we gave each other weary hugs goodbye. I thanked him for the experience, for the specialness of it, for taking me to a wooded kingdom, where I was happy to reign as queen, if only for a couple of days.

ARMAND GARNET RUFFO

WRITING THE WATER

The water brought me here. For as long as I can remember rivers and lakes have been integral to my life. Among my earliest childhood memories is one of piling into a boat and travelling for what seemed like days to get to that special fishing spot. Later that evening the stars and moon sprinkling the shoreline with light would guide us home. I think of this because the Anishnaabe have always been a people of the water. Our rituals come to mind, the sound of the water-drum. One of our earliest stories is of a giant turtle rising from the depths and becoming home, hence the name 'Turtle Island' for the land we now share. Between hills of spruce, glades of birch, walls of granite squeezed to the surface when the earth was young, the lakes and rivers have always given the Anishnaabe both sustenance and pleasure. In turn, we have come to honour the significance of this life-force and pray that it will continue in a good way.

I come to this conclusion (or is it a beginning?) as the floating dock I am lying on shifts, and I feel myself carried by the undulating waves. I sit up and look out across the darkened water. Two o'clock in the morning, and the music of the bush blowing off the lake engulfs me. I look back to the light. The old timers are still at it, still talking about times when I was wet behind the ears, lamenting now that almost everyone is gone. I tell myself that tomorrow I will go over to the graveyard, stand in the tall weeds, amid the toppled and rotting markers, and greet my relations. Moments ago I heard a howl that lifted me up and carried me out the door and across the damp grass. Now, as I lay on the dock looking out to the dark space, I realize I have wanted, no needed to write about this lake for a long time. Probably all my life.

The journey began this morning when Buck took me and my cousin out to Indian Lake to see our great grandfather's trapping cabin. The same cabin where he hid Archie Belaney, better known as Grey Owl, the Englishman turned Indian, out from the law. As the story goes, Archie had one too many and started throwing knives at passing trains. Upset with Belaney's shenanigans, the CPR Operator wired the town of Chapleau for a police officer to come and arrest him. The warrant reads, "Unlawful conduct in a disorderly manner whilst drunk at the Biscotasing Railway Station." It's something the old timers used to laugh about. I documented this while writing about Belaney in my book <u>Grey Owl: The Mystery of Archie Belaney</u>. Perhaps a better way to say it is that I imagined this into my book. But, no, that's not entirely true because it did happen. The cabin is still standing as testimony.

Floating, listening to the whisked voices rise from the house, the lamp light spread in my direction, I remember a wise man once telling me, in a voice I might have heard a hundred years ago, that you cannot be part of anything. You either are or are not. And I looked at his polished cane cut from the root of a tree, which he tapped down to rise slowly. His observation comes to me now and makes me ask that if you are part of something what does that entail? And what if you are not? Are you liberated? Or burdened by loss? The dock moves, and I think that perhaps it has become unmoored and has floated back to the cabin. Not to the place I visited earlier today, but to where my great grandfather is still living seventy years ago. I float towards him. He is wearing dark wool pants, a blue flannel shirt rolled up at the sleeves, red underwear peeking out. He looks exactly like the man in the black and white photographs my grandmother has shown me time and time again. To each photograph, she has attached a story which she attaches to me, as though it were my place to remember.

He is repairing the cabin roof, the same roof that was about to cave in this morning. He stops to wave like he knows me and beacons me to land. I can see that he is happy to see me.

"Great-grandfather," I call, "*Auneen.*"

"I've been waiting for you," he says.

Then, in a blink of my eye, he is in front of me clasping my hand to help me up the steep embankment.

I look to the roof and back to him. I'm about to ask him how he managed to get down so quickly when he asks me if I'd like a good cup of bush-tea.

"Sure," I say, and the steaming drink is instantly in my hand.

"Not like you saw it earlier is it?" he says, glancing back to the cabin.

The logs look newly peeled. But how? How many ways to travel on water? This morning I needed a guide. It was raining, and I thought Buck might decide to cancel the trip. Lake Biscotasing is part of a huge water system containing hundreds of islands, its southern arm flowing into an equally huge Indian Lake. Even with Buck's big boat it takes hours to get from lake to lake. But no, nine o'clock on the dot and he was calling to ask if my cousin and I were ready to go. He said he had lots of raincoats. Besides a little rain wouldn't melt us. Half hour later, we were on the lake. Hence the whiskey. We knew he wouldn't take money because he kept telling us that the cabin is our heritage, our history, and he thought he should bring us there. We wanted to show him our appreciation and a bottle of the best seemed like a reasonable response. We didn't realize he would insist that we share in the festivities that were to follow. A few other locals showed up after we returned and out with the drink came the stories. There was no way I could leave.

I don't have any desire to throw knives at passing trains, though I must say after a couple of drinks the lake looks so inviting I'm tempted to jump in and float away. Up to the stars reflecting like tiny fires on the surface of the water, as I try to understand what the trip to the cabin means to me. I see the arc of that first moment when I pushed open the old plank door, crossed the threshold and found myself standing in the past. What I'm trying to say is that my going there has something to do with voice, something to do with the voices still there, not there, something to do with my voice. By this I'm referring to the place where for a brief instant I saw past meet present, and I was part of it, part of its shape, because it included me and my moment in its construction. In a sense I see it in the arc of my great-grandfather's hammer, my first step from the boat onto the embankment, my first push of the door, the shape of all those things that have contributed to who I am and how I interpret the world. For me, on that rainy Thursday, I was not merely at my great-grandfather's cabin, I was the cabin, and it was me. This may sound strange, but I cannot think of a better way to say it.

To look at it, it's not much, a small single room trapper's cabin made of logs and rough squared timber. The back butts up to the hillside where the tar paper roof is beginning to topple in. The front is a mere few feet from the water's edge. Inside, the floor consists of a few heavy planks, now moldy and rotting, laying loose on the bare ground. There is a rough bed frame made of spruce, a small plank table beside a small window that lets in the bare minimum of light. A practical place, where my great-grandfather sought shelter while doing the rounds on his trapping ground. I cannot fail to see that the same place where Archie Grey Owl also sought shelter has become, over the years, shelter for fishermen, hunters, sightseers and even maintenance workers from the hydro dam. The tell-tale signs, the litter of rusted cans and the various dates and names (some of whom I recognize) carved into the log walls.

I am brought to the stories of my grandmother who tells me of going out with her father and helping him as only a ten year old can. One time spring broke early, the weather turned warm so quickly they couldn't walk on the ice and nearly starved to death. Luckily it turned cold again, and they managed to make it out to the village for a few basic supplies like flour and salt pork. "We were strong in them days," she likes to say, "good food, good water." I think of the photograph she gave me of herself standing with her parents outside the cabin, beaver pelts stretched on the walls. And yet trapping was only my great-grandfather's winter occupation. By spring he was once again an outfitter, guiding tourists from as far away as the United States and Europe. His own father, a Chief of the

Eshkemanetigon (Spanish River) First Nation, he had believed a whiteman's education was necessary for the future and had sent his son to a seminary in Montreal. As long as my grandmother remembers, her father always had a subscription to both La Presse and The Globe. Taken in 1932, the photograph shows my great-grandfather standing proudly with his young family, a mere four years before his death. And I am led to wonder how different life would have been for his family had he lived. What shape would I live today?

"Great-grandfather," I say, "this is the cabin you brought Archie Belaney, isn't it?"

"Would you like to see the inside?"

He turns toward the door, and I am at the threshold. The first thing I notice is that everything is so neat, everything has its place. And bright. Such a stark contrast to the dark dank room I saw earlier this morning.

"He wrote over there." He points to the little plank table in front of the window.

"Always took lots of notes about everything."

"How long did he stay?"

"About three months, and then he came back to Bisco to say goodbye and left."

"But he eventually returned?"

"Yes, when he became Grey Owl."

"He missed the place."

"As it was. Not what it was becoming."

A boat passes by in the distance and wakes me. I have been dreaming. Drifting.

The dock rocks, the sky expands into a galaxy of stars as waves lap the shoreline and disperse the sand. Dispersed. That's what I've been looking to say. That's us. A few years ago, I decided to drive down to the reserve where I still have a few relatives. New houses were going up. Families who had lost their status because of marrying either non-natives or non-status were moving back with their families (now that Bill C31 had been ratified.) As I drove around, I wondered how the newcomers would be received? Then I turned onto Espaniel Street named after our family. For a moment I felt a sense of elation in the knowledge that a hundred years ago my relatives had been the original signatories to the treaty which set aside land for the reserve. After that initial moment, however, I remembered that only part of our family had moved down to live on the reserve.

As the story goes, two brothers moved and took part of the clan with them. A third brother, our side of the family, refused to leave his home for a reserve hundreds of miles away, refused to give up his ability to live off his own land. The price of freedom had been dear. Although he petitioned for help for his people, and reserve status for their own land, it was denied, and the village became overrun with foreigners. The government's policy of attrition and assimilation prevailed. The Canadian Pacific Railway opened the area and brought in an influx of settlers and trappers who readily claimed title to land that the Aboriginal people had lived on for generations. The lumber barons of the time also moved in. Those like J.R. Booth and E.B. Eddie claimed vast cutting rights, and with political influence, there was no stopping them. The huge operations themselves employed hundreds of men and provided jobs for the influx of new immigrants, not to mention a solid tax base for an ever expanding country. The woodlands were simply a resource to be cut and exploited. Once in a letter, dated 1884, to the visiting Superintendent of Indian Affairs, my great-grandfather's own father, Chief Sahquakegick, voiced his distress:

"All of my old people who used to hunt near here are in great need. The construction of the Canadian Pacific Railway has opened up the country in the neighbourhood of Lake Pogamasing to White Trappers who deprive the Indians of the Beaver, which they carefully preserved, never taking all, but leaving some to increase, and as the Whites kill and destroy all they can, the consequences will be that no Beaver will be left in that section of the country."

Like so many others, it was a letter that fell on deaf ears. Indians were simply not part of the master narrative for Canada. To put it another way, Indians were a nuisance, an anachronism in the way of progress and were expected to fade away.

Along with the loss of land went the sense of collectivity rooted in that land. With the passing of the Elders, the younger generation found themselves bound to the assimilative policies of the day. Enfranchisement became common practice so that Aboriginal people could find gainful employment. The only problem was very few white Canadians would hire Indians. Status, non-status, Métis, it was all the same to them. War broke out (three times counting Korea) and the men signed up in droves to escape the poverty. At least with a cheque from the army their families wouldn't starve. Many didn't return. They were either buried abroad or upon their return moved to cities and towns to find work. Many ended up on the street. What all this means is that there are no longer Anishnaabe campfires on this traditional gathering place my family once called home. No longer Anishnaabe voices. Aboriginal tradition has been lost here as it has elsewhere in Canada. The voices of my ancestors lament this passing. Tonight I listen to them.

They tell me of being herded into schools that attempted to destroy the spirit of a people. It is now well documented that the government and the clergy did everything in their power to destroy Aboriginal people both as individuals and as a collectivity. To quote Duncan Campbell Scott, Deputy Superintendent General of Indian Affairs, and architect of the Residential School system, his policies were designed to "get rid of the Indian problem." Little wonder that Aboriginal people suffer from a legacy of what is now termed "social dysfunction." Take my own uncles and aunties, take those of nearly every Anishnaabe in this country, we all have family lost to the street, dead before their time. Tonight I honour them with prayers and tears and look to the stars on the water to show me another way. A breeze rustles the poplar trees around the shore, and then there is a sudden calmness. There is beauty in the land. No matter what happens it will survive. I think of the history of existence on our Earth Mother, and we humans are but infants with infantile behaviour.

Again I rise to the surface of consciousness. The buzz of the boat has nearly faded into the morning. I wonder who it could be? A few years ago it seemed like it took forever to get here. At one time there was only the waterways and the lake served as a site for a Hudson Bay Company post where my relations came to sell their furs. For the longest time it remained isolated and relatively unscathed. But with the railroad and logging, expanding into today's multinational billion dollar business, came a network of roads and clear-cuts that has spread across the land like a blight. Everybody and everything moving so fast, becoming so efficiently mechanized, they are now cutting a few kilometers away from the lake. Over the last twenty years folks from Sudbury and southern Ontario have also begun to claim the lake for cottage country. Just around the next bay an American couple run Grey Owl Camps, a local tourist outfit, the kind of work my great-grandfather did some sixty years ago. He would chuckle if he heard the name. Once, under a newer moon, he opened a letter from Archie Belaney and found it signed Grey Owl.

"Were you surprised?" I ask him between sips of tea.

"Not really." He says, sitting down against a birch tree.

"You helped him?"

"We all did. Mostly everybody, I mean Indian people now."

"Why didn't you say anything?"

"Because he'd learned good and was doing good and that was good enough for us."

"That's what it was about, wasn't it?"

"That's all it's ever about. Besides he made us laugh, all that hooting of his!"

"There were reporters who wanted to expose him."

"Sure there were, but nobody asked us. Back then we didn't exist. Least not in a real way."

"Though that one from North Bay finally asked his first wife."

"That's right, after I passed on."

"And everything changed," I am about to say, when the mention of death brings me back to the water. I dip my hand into the lake's cool surface. The dream again. I sit up on the dock, and he is gone. I am alone, on the water, among the stars. I promise myself that next year I will canoe out to my great-grandfather's cabin for one last visit. I'm not sure why. Maybe, it's because I feel the need to travel close to the water, to extend the journey into one long slow goodbye. For certain it is not to say goodbye to who I am. Quite the opposite. I would even go so far to say it is this last physical remnant of where we once stood that has confirmed who I am. For it has given me a place from which to build, and I doubt it would be any different were I visiting a castle rather than an old decaying cabin. I listen to the departing voices, the last few old timers going home. There will come a time, in the not too distant future, when they too will be silenced. As for my home, I carry it inside me now, as the cabin disappears into the earth, as the lake carries on, for this, in the end, is who I am.

RUSSELL TEED

FATHER

The Fall
September 1971

I'm a nine-year-old boy and I sit up on the rocks, under a windsock behind my house, down in old town. I know my dad is gone, but it doesn't seem real to me. Nothing seems real to me now. Even the tiny goosebumps all over my body do not feel real. There's no sun today, but I'm sweating. I think it's Monday. I'm not certain if today is even the same day. I saw a big yellow stripe on that policeman's pant leg, but that was some time ago. He stood in the doorway, and that's when I realized that my goosebumps changed. They never felt that way before in the cold September wind. I cried in my auntie's arms. I don't know why. I remember thinking about why I was crying, and about why I was thinking. I'm hot. I can't see the sun. There's no sun. I'm shivering. I saw the sun Friday. It crashed on the horizon. There weren't any flames, just clouds of grey smoke. They're still everywhere, grey clouds. They'll always be everywhere unless I can heal. They wisp across grey skies and through the branches of Weeping Willows. They're Birch trees... Weeping Willows. Spruce trees... Weeping Willows. Pine trees... They're all Weeping Willows to me. Their tears flow down the rocky cliffs in front of me. They carry Eagles and warriors and mothers and children. They flood the back bay of Great Slave Lake. And the wind blows out of control from the North. Whitecaps come from where his boat flipped over. From where he was sent into the wet, dry mid-point between cold and hot, between disbelief and distraught. From the North over lakes, over land, white caps roll closer, faster, whiter, colder until ice covers the entire North, and the wind freezes my heart so callous it cracks and breaks into frigid splinters. The river of tears that flows carries them chattering down those rocky cliffs in front of my body. I sit at the highest point of rock. If his soul is in the sky I want to be near it. I look up as my heart continues to splinter and fall down, down, chattering down. I sift through grey clouds hoping to see the sun shine through my bedroom window into my sleep-filled eyes. And desperately hoping to see him standing in front of my hollow body, I hold my hands cupped on either side of my face so to hide the emptiness this world has to offer me. And the clouds fade into the shadows that my hands cast upon myself. From the shadows I can hear him. I can smell him. I can see him, but his face is distorted. From the shadows I can hear the spring ice in the Yellowknife River. I can see it as it chatters and flows, bumping together. I dive in and swim deep where the sun shines and the skies are blue. I hear the Jingle Dress dancer and I see her skip along in a warm mid-summer breeze. She's smiling before me, and her feet fall at different angles in front of me, and I hear her dress make it's chattering sounds with each different step. I smile at her, but she just keeps on dancing. Her dress sounds just like the spring ice. And I realize it's not the spring ice that I hear. And I realize it's not the Jingle Dress dancer that I hear. I struggle to the surface and gasp for air. But I don't open my eyes. I'm too scared to lower my hands, because I don't want to forget him. I can still vaguely hear his voice. And I can still smell him. But his face is really distorted now, and it shrivels and it withers to nothing. I open my eyes. My smile shatters and joins the truth, the splinters of my frozen heart chattering down rocky cliffs in the river of tears. It hurts inside and the cold wind blows through me. It takes my childhood and almost all my endurance away. And here I sit, a shell, a child, empty and alone with only faith left to guide me. I'm a nine-year old boy sitting under a windsock.

This Cold Midnight Sun
Winter 1981

I'm guiding you down a gravel highway. Thin scales of snow fall and line the gutter. I'm the Midnight Sun caught in a cycle, seemingly lost in a frozen track just above the horizon, masking the stars with my ominous facade of power, wavering beams, relentless feigns of crippling heat rays. I push at your thin skin, making you weak, yet making your hide thick, beating down on the back of your neck, working my way into your mind, forcing your head down. Your arms try to deflect my pulsating numbness, but I become your thoughts. I rage within my own eyes and gain strength. In my mind, I am a Sun, growing bright red from pink, expanding into blazing gold layers that vibrate and surround me, around true yellow masquerading across, what I see as, a shrivelling sky. I'm a confused spider feeding on its own pod that it has shed in the night. You shudder unknowing, and I push you to the shoulder into the dust and snowflakes that mold your mind, making our thoughts one. My one. A one-way highway controlled by a green plastic cap that smothers the yellow light that leaks through cracks inside me. I'm the Midnight Sun, the red faced one, and into a ditch of drying cracked mud, I lead you. All the signs bring you further down. Legs struggle to stand, but a face first shove sends you into the deep. You come up fast, out of control, your lungs reaching for fuel. Saliva and tears streak and crystallize over the mask I've shaped around you. I have your hair in my fingers. Scratching at the roots, my forged rays blister your scalp, and for a moment I'm lost in the fantasy of total control. Power seems to flash in my hands' grasp, bringing me full circle. A dysfunctionalist's twisted thought of completion, a climactic Heavenly Hell. But a breeze sways us and blows between us, breaking my hold. The moment gone. True yellow fades fool's gold, and I see the welts on your heart, and I feel them sting mine. I breathe in deep the searing stress that I've conjured. Fire liqufies my eyes. Frozen flames of blue spray from my charcoal heart, scouring your mask from pale to chrome. I see myself in that hardened shell, that mirror's reflection. I see myself for the first time and I hear clearly the echoes of truth when my shriek deflects off the transparent wall that encases your cold dark eyes. I can see my breath. I shiver as you rise gaining your much-needed strength back, though remaining cold as I. I fall into the snowflakes and dust. I squirm rippling along the horizon while the clouds build around me, through me. Thunder scolds my abrasive rind and darkness floods from behind me and inside me. Hail pummels into snowflakes' mist. I become a shadow, a chilled thought, lost and blowing in the North wind biting at hands and freezing hearts. I become the snapping wind whipping across drifts of crusted snow, across faces of leather. I am the Ice cracking crying and moaning, shifting unsettled, realizing the DREAM of warm radiant laughter, of heartfelt hugs and kisses are but only a frozen nightmare buried in a coffin deep in layers of pain and self-hate that seems destined never to thaw in this cold Midnight Sun.

The Thaw
April 1991

I remember when he was here with me, the smile he smiled anywhere, everywhere.

And I can hear my name. It's him in the grey clouds I feel, I smell. I remember the way he looked, his hair black as the Raven who reminds me of the day he walked into the shadow of Raven's breath. And the birds that got caught and died quickly under the heavy metal wash basin had something to sing about. He, who helped bury them, joined them in song, his song. And all the little babies cried. The babies cried. Without speaking, in mother's arms, they cried, on a tear stained picture that wrinkled and faded deeper into black skies. A lightning flash, only a reflection crashed on a reef in time. Years went by. They went by faster and faster. And the years went by fast, whirled with wind, lost together with gray haired people's memories. They were only visions crushed by Raven picking eyeballs from leathered skin, indifferent to where those eyes were and the places they had been and seen, the places he had been, with eyes dried like mine, sunk in. My heart has shrivelled to a frigid stone and heaved from frozen chest. A crystal cast, spinning into a river of dreams. It is reflection. It is as a tear drop drowned in echoed sorrowed calls of a sparrow, a sparrow, a sparrow flying into evening shades, into halls and walls and wash basins unevening vast pictures of past futures of mirrored snowbirds set free in perpetual drift. I remember the Snowbirds pulling my soul thread until one last strand of spirit skin stretched, unravelling and unveiled in front of me, almost forever. Finally a slight tearing and it pulled and lifted upward with a delicate gasp, deflating, descending down between North wind's breaths to where his remains were at rest, abandoned. Now, just as sun's rays, he lays faded, forgotten by his own surroundings, buried, waiting within thin layers of sediment to weather away, a memory to be released, his soul to soar up through, over and around Aurora, dancing and again, in dream, in distant reflection, in thought, in tears. He is with me once more.

Warming Embrace
July 1996

I see the smiles they wear. I can't explain how they make me feel and my heart beat. I can't explain the cries and tears. I can't explain my thoughts, my reflections, the cycle I ride. I'm watching life begin. I'm watching growth. I'm watching the past mature. I'm watching the future take hold. I'm watching the present calm. Blood memories forming within; story flowing through tiny veins and I see ordinary things. They mean so much to me now. I see fingers, only fingers. I see toes, they're only toes. I see a pair of noses. I see eyes, oh those eyes. I see them watch me. But I see more than only fingers. I see more than only toes. I see more than their noses.I see more than their eyes. I see more than one child. I see more than children. I see my eyes. I see my toes. I see my fingers. I see my nose. I see my eyes, no longer leather. My little girl and boy show me life. I haven't seen life for so long. I've never known what it was because it was taken and I scratched away, away, away. To live! I've never known what it was like to grow from the heart. Ice. It's been so cold waiting for the sun's truth to warm and send me strength. My little girl and boy show me growth, in them, in me, in sunshine, warmth and the memories, reflecting, dancing in the rays warming my thoughts of sad times. They make me breathe. They make me smile. They make me feel my heart beat. They make me think where we come from. They make me think of family, my father, dancing in the heat, free in a thought once more. I'm growing with them. I'm growing for them. I'm growing into the person they need me to be. I'm growing into the father they can depend on. I'm growing into the father they can respect. I'm growing into the father I need to be. I'm growing into the father that I can depend on. I'm growing into the father I can respect. I'm growing into their father. I'm growing into my father.

I'm a nine year old boy!
I'm guiding you down a gravel highway!
I remember when he was with me, the smile he smiled anywhere, everywhere!
I see the smiles they wear!

RICHARD VAN CAMP

25 ALBUMS THAT SAVED MY LIFE

Ladies and gentlemen, it is my sincere pleasure to bring to you my list of the top twenty-five albums I have ever had the joy of listening to:

1. <u>Prince – Purple Rain</u> I think I was fourteen at the time, but I do remember a horrified Marnie Martin working at the drug store in Fort Smith, NWT, going, "Can you believe they can print lyrics like that on the cover of a record jacket?" I read the lyrics for *When Doves Cry* on the record jacket and bought it immediately. I had seen the video and thought Prince looked like a naked monkey with sideburns sitting in his bathtub, yet really loved his band and him (when clothed) dancing around. I was always scared he'd slip and fall and twist something in those heels, but he pulled it off all right. When Marnie raised her voice in protest about the lyrics she raised my interest in Prince. I already had *1999* and knew Prince was a highly charged sexual force, yet nothing prepared me for *Purple Rain*. I think this album is the one that launched my passion for music.

2. <u>Kate Bush – Hounds of Love</u> Saw the video for *Running up That Hill* and fainted. Ran to the same drug store in Smith and, (Thank You God!) it was in stock. Ran home across the potato field, flew to my room and put it on. I lay there for days in a daze. I love Kate Bush's ability to stuff novels, anecdotes, ideas, moments of her life into songs. Anyone who has seen the video for *Experiment IV* or meditated on her near-dance with Hitler in *Heads We're Dancing* knows what I mean. Where are you now, Kate?

3. <u>Platinum Blonde – Standing in the Dark.</u> I saw the video for *Standing in the Dark* and loved the look, loved the lyrics, loved the hair! I bought the album at

the drug store (probably a few days after *Purple Rain* and *Hounds of Love* came in) and knew something had changed deeply inside me. All of their albums are superb and I miss them. I was babysitting in those days and would listen to *Standing in the Dark* over and over while reading "True Crime" magazines, which seemed to be all the rage in the early eighties. I remember babysitting one winter, reading an article about a serial killer who shaved the pubic hair off all of his victims with a straight razor after binding them to their beds before feeding on them. The song playing as I read this was *Cast No Shadows*. I still get that "alone in the dark" feeling whenever I hear it. That tape became my soundtrack for terror lacing itself with horrible images of crime photos of bedsheets and bloodstains. I was so scared I made myself watch "Good Rocking Tonight" on CBC. Eddie Grant's *Electric Avenue* video was really the only thing that stopped me from running home screaming through ice fog at two in the morning without my jacket or shoes.

4. <u>Van Halen – 1984</u> I was listening to this in Grade Eight along with every other mammal on the planet. I could feel the rock and cockiness of the band and began my secret career as an air drummer in my bedroom. Most males hop around the room playing their leg like a guitar but I chose the drums as my vent. It didn't take a genius to know I was in the presence of a great United States of America Kick Ass Rock and Roll Band before falling victim to my glorious teenage years. Who was better—Sammy Haggar or David Lee Roth? Who cares? Both lead singers took the band and its fans to heights never achieved before by any hard rock band.

5. <u>Cindy Lauper – She's So Unusual</u> My childhood ended with this album in Grade Nine. My buddy Lorne was sleeping over one night and received a phone call from his hysterical mother who was screaming that his father, Sandy, went missing. She was sure that when he was cutting wood he must have fallen through the ice. She was sending a friend to pick us up so we could look for Sandy. Sandy's friend was a paramedic of some kind.

I brought *She's So Unusual* along thinking that if we were going to find a body we had better have some "happy" music. Well, fuck, Cindy turned on me. Sandy's friend, Mr. Paramedic, began telling us stories of all of the bodies he's ever found. *She's So Unusual*, over the course of one of the most terrifying evenings of my life, became my soundtrack for body-hunting. Whenever I listen to it now, I see a white face opening black eyes as it rises out of cold dark water. I never, ever should have brought that tape along because we listened to it seven complete times while driving through a long cold forty-below night. We learned, after almost losing our own lives to the highway graders, that Sandy, hours earlier, caught a ride home from another pal of his and was safely tucked away in bed

By the way, in *All Through the Night* I thought for years Cindy was singing, "We have no cats/ we want respect/please hit me forward all through the night" when she was really singing, "We have no past/ we won't reach back/ keep with me forward all through the night." But that's not as retarded as my buddy Trevor who thought the Police were singing, "There is no milk for our Chee-ri-os" instead of "We are spirits in the material world." But you know what? That's not half as bad as Andy C. who thought Sting was singing "I'll always be King of Spain" instead of "King of Pain". Try and figure that one out!

6. Depeche Mode – Violator   Listening to this in Grade Twelve when Luke Oskirko, who I think may be dead now, moved to Fort Smith. I cruised to this tape so much I went through three of them before buying the disc, which was eventually stolen from me. I could direct a thousand videos based on the visuals I get from each song, especially *Waiting for the Night*. DM's *Blue Dress* is written and sung with such a polite ferocity and with such a disturbing Lolita message I still get the chills whenever I hear it: "Because when you learn/ you'll know what makes the world turn."

7. Eurythmics – Touch   I tried being a pothead between the grades of nine and ten. Each time I was stoned, I seemed to end up back in my loft lying on the floor listening to this album. Even when I listen to it now I get these great flashbacks of one night the power being out, my family visiting beneath me in the living room, and little stoned me lying on my back in the loft floating around the room via candlelight. I was always a little spooked by David Smith in their videos, especially

Love is a Stranger. I've since surrendered all awe to him and Annie but remember my days of doubt as I inhaled sweet mojo through a toilet paper roll over red hot stove elements.

8. <u>Fine Young Cannibals – Fine Young Cannibals</u> Saw the video for *Johnny Come on Home* and was a little alarmed at the band's stage show: Two strange white guys dancing awkwardly not smiling while this dark boy gave it all away dancing on his knees begging for Johnny to come on home. I ran across the potato field immediately to a new store in town called "The Video Store" and (Thank God again!) it was in stock. I bought it on the spot and this is the 911 dramatization of the conversation I had with the lady owner who went out of business one week later.

Owner: Fine Young Cannibals? That's a strange name for a band. Are they, like, Death Metal?

RVC (hyper-ventilating): Aw, man. Aw, man, you haven't heard of them? You know that song, Johnny, we're sorry, come on home?

Owner: No. No, I can't say that I have.

RVC (still hyperventilating): Aw, man, you will—YOU WILL!!

I ran home and put it on and started dancing on my knees just like the lead singer. Fuck, I was so cool back then! If you watch all of FYC's videos those white boys never crack smiles—ever.

9. <u>Pearl Jam – 10</u> My folks were out of town. Someone, I won't say who, was fooling around with his girlfriend in our log house in Fort Smith. She had just returned from the city with the disc. I saw Pearl Jam's video for *Even Flow* and had discounted the velocity of the band based on Eddie Vedder's potato hair. The lovers in question turned up the tunes so I couldn't listen to them go "straight erogenous" (my words, not theirs). Thank God they did because I left my body that night. Vedder's resonating voice and Pearl Jam's velocity stole my soul. I

taped it the next morning and listened to it over and over before they woke up.

10. <u>The Cure – Disintegration</u> I saw the video for *Fascination Street* in the spring of 1989 and wind-sprinted all the way to downtown Calgary yelling at the top of my lungs. I didn't know an album could actually pull my spirit from my body and show me heaven so fast. I was listening to it when I graduated from William Aberhart High School in Calgary where I did my Grade Twelve. I must say, though, that I return to their *Faith* album a lot more than *Disintegration* so we may have a tie. Either way, *Disintegration* gets my vote for the best-written album of all time.

11. <u>Sisters of Mercy – (Tie!) First and Last and Always and Floodland</u> Now because the band broke up to reform as The Mission and The Sisters of Mercy (and, briefly as The Sisterhood), I think I'll choose an album before and after The Breakup. Before The Breakup, I would have to say *First and Last and Always* because every song is pure Goth. Why this album meant so much to me was because I was working at McDonalds in Calgary making $4.20 an hour. I loved the lyrics and loved Andrew Eldritch's deep, drowning voice. I loved the mystery behind the Goth movement. I loved how The Sisters stood backlit by searchlights six feet back from the stage surrounded by fog. Used and abused, I'd lay there at 7 AM eating my McMuffin, sipping my McCoffee, saving my McHashbrown for last, smiling away in the darkened staff room with a shiny forehead and a Rudolph nose blaring The Sisters. I was actually pretty lame back then. I'd wear my black "Fuck Me and Marry Me Young" Sisters' shirt under my McUniform and think I was a McSomebody. What a fool! I was crushed for a second when I found out The Sisters split up. I say "for a second' because both bands went on to do beautiful work. The Mission's *Wasteland* and *Children* were awesome, but never touched me as deeply as The Sisters.

After The Breakup, I would have to say The Sisters' best album was *Floodland* because it is so well written with heart and soul. You can really feel Andrew Eldritch mourning the loss of something deep inside. Check out *Driven by the Snow* and try not to see people buried by snow.

I learned ten years later that *1959* was recorded by Andrew Eldritch after a fan named "Isabelle" wrote to the lead singer and suggested he record a song with only a piano and his voice. Isn't that just class? One of the best albums ever written. I will always be a slave to the Sisters.

12. <u>Ministry – The Land of Rape and Honey</u> Bought it from the cover alone in 1989. I had no idea what ferocity would be unleashed inside me when I opened her up. The second I head Alan Jourgenson sing, "Stronger than reason/ Stronger than lies/ The only truth I know is the look in your eyes…" I knew I could never go back to anything I believed in before. In fact, it was this album that spilled my cocaine glands and lit my rat brain on fire. This led to my dangerous friendship with Skinny Puppy, Hilt, Revolting Cocks, Nine Inch Nails, Front 242 and Chris and Cosey. Chris and Cosey, by the way, suck. I wasted so much money trying to find anything beautiful about them. I saw one video of theirs and was a sucker for years trying to find the track to that video. Anyways, If you've never heard the Revolting Cocks'(the Ministry's sister band) cover for Rod Stewart's "If You Think I'm Sexy" and Olivia Newton John's "Let's Get Physical" you have not lived.

I want to say that the Ministry's following album *The Mind is a Terrible Thing to Taste* is also brilliant. *Dream Song* will always haunt me. Do I believe in angels? You're fucking rights I do after I heard this song.

13. <u>The Smiths – Strangeways, Here We Come</u> I can't remember what exactly turned me on to The Smiths. Maybe it was the fact that they were not Top Forty or maybe it was Morrissey's great hair. Who knows? All I know is the second I heard *Last Night I Dreamt That Somebody Loved Me* I was hooked. I ended up getting everything they ever did and even followed Morrissey's career when he went solo. I never knew a man could take his voice to such beautiful places. I challenge anyone to listen to the Smith's *Hatful of Hollow* and try not to disappear inside themselves and return with a heavy heart and a prayer on one's lips after hearing: *Back to the Old House, Real Around the Fountain* and *Please, Please, Please, Let Me Get What I Want*. On his own, *Viva Hate* was by far Morrissey's best. What a voice! What a band!

14. <u>The Modern Lovers – The Modern Lovers</u> This was the soundtrack for my year studying Land Claims in Yellowknife. I had heard Jonathan Richman sing *Pablo Picasso* one late night on CBC's "Brave New Waves" and ordered it through Yellowknife's Sam the Record Man. I love Jonathan Richman and was so disappointed with anything he did before or after this album. He looked so sick years later in *There's Something About Mary* and wished he'd never have appeared in the movie. Everything's so right with this one album, though, and can't blame him for trying to reach the level of genius he achieved with this one. He was so horny and lonely when he recorded it and it sounds like someone's just broke his nose. Jonathan speaks for every fucking guy who's ever lived!

15. <u>Iggy Pop – Blah Blah Blah</u> When I saw the video for *Cry For Love* I fell to the earth and started moaning. Here was Iggy Pop, a man who had obviously seen better days, dancing like a weirdo and looking great doing it. I had to have the album. When I listened to it I sensed immediately that I was in the presence of a true artist who had just put out a collection of songs that were dear to him. I liked how he could kick my ass with *Winners and Losers* and yet sing so tenderly in a track like *Shades*. It's an awesome album. Years later, I thought he made an ass of himself with Blondie and their *Did You Ever?* video and later with his *Lust for Life* track off the Trainspotting Soundtrack, but this is one of my all time favorite albums.

16. <u>Fleetwood Mac – Rumours</u> I was always scared of Mick Fleetwood's glass balls on the cover, yet I love the look in Stevie Nick's face. A great album: I believe their finest. I had seen it in everyone's house and home but never really listened to it until my first year in college in Yellowknife. I had escaped a landlady who was damn ripping me off and had called in a favour from a friend to let me stay at her apartment. She was madly in love and agreed: she was never there anyway. I played it one late summer night while having a bath and couldn't believe how timeless the entire album was. I heard *Songbird* and left my body, swam around the universe for awhile, and came home shivering but happy.

17. <u>Beastie Boys – Use Your Head</u> I can't even listen to this anymore because it's tattooed in nodules across my brain. I listened to this tape a thousand times while at the En'owkin International School of Writing. I could feel all the hard work and focus The Boys put into every song. It's like they knew that LP would either make them or break them. I think this album made them men and they felt and knew it too.

18. <u>Cocteau Twins – Tiny Dynamine/Echoes in a Shallow Bay</u> Man, where do I even begin with these three angels? I was working for the Dene Nation in Yellowknife in their Health Department one summer. I was sent to Ottawa upon the second day of my employment for a meeting about the Brighter Futures initiative. I took notes and was supposed to keep my mouth shut, but instead ended up telling everyone what a great job they were doing and how proud I was of them. I'm sure they thought I was developmentally delayed. Anyhow, I walked into a head shop/tape shop and asked the scariest guy there what the most beautiful music in the world was. He said immediately, "Cocteau Twins" and found their tape *Heaven or Las Vegas* for me. I listened to it but didn't care for it; however, I was drawn to one song: *Frou-frou Foxes in Midsummer Fires*. Although Elizabeth Frazer did not sing in any language, I could feel what she was trying to say. When I listened to it over and over (much to the alarm of my mother who thought I was smoking up again), I remembered an interview I had read between the Cure and HMV in which I learned that Robert Smith listened to nothing but Cocteau Twins during the making of *Disintegration*. Well, that was it. I had to hear what he heard and feel what he felt. I ended up buying *Tiny Dynamine* and listening to it tens of thousands of times never getting enough. They do create the best music in the world. One reporter confessed she had "Eargasms" listening to them and I really wish the world would discover them as deeply as Michelle and I have. This tape saved my life when I worked at a bush camp outside of Yellowknife and was miserable for a thousand reasons. My wife and I have since collected just about everything they have ever done including their box set, which is strategically placed by the door in case of fire, locust attack or twister.

19. <u>Tragically Hip – Fully and Completely</u> I heard this one night cruising with my crew on a Fort Smith Christmas break and felt for the first time like my own man. Gordon Downie took the band above some Canadian freakshow and launched them internationally. I don't see the shine in them anymore the way I did with that album. Downie's lyrics are so full of the poetic mystery. I saw him once at the Vancouver airport. He just looked pissed off. It was 7 AM and I'm sure I didn't look any better. What a wizard!

20. <u>Slowdive – Souvlaki</u> This is a soundtrack for my first year at UVIC. I heard a song one midnight in Penticton at the Green Bean Café and went running into the kitchen begging the waitress to let me borrow the tape so I could hear this song again. She did. She even called the waiter who made the mix and hummed a few verses of the song to find out the name of the band. I got mixed up and bought Slowburn which sucked and thought maybe I was retarded for about six months while working for CBC's TV series "North of 60" until one day I found Slowdive at A&B Sound and picked it up. When I listened to it, I could not believe the harmonics and melodies of the group. They were so young yet knew how to take me away from the taxman and any guilt I had ever felt about anything. They produced another great album, *Just for A Day,* which almost measures up to *Souvlaki*. I know the technology will never be available to come even near the video I would love to make for their song *Allison*. Incidentally, Slowdive broke up after only five years and formed Mojave 3, which sucks. Anyone dying for gorgeous music? I bring you Slowdive.

21. <u>Cranes – Forever</u> Here I thought I had escaped that "looking for a body in the darkest of winter with only a headlight and a handgun" feeling until I heard this awesome band. Lead singer, Alison Shaw, uses the voice of a little girl to haunt you while her brother, James, and the other Cranes rock you. Music to find bodies to… for everyone.

22. <u>The Smashing Pumpkins – Mellon Collie and the Infinite Sadness</u> Saw the video for *Bullet with Butterfly Wings* and did a back flip! Ran to A&B Sound in Victoria and knew I was standing in the way of something huge and fierce. They

Pumpkins could have gotten away with any one of the two discs in the set and they would have still lit me on fire. Anything from them before or after this project bores me; however, they blessed a year of my life in university. In fact, I would say it was the soundtrack for my second year at UVIC.

23. <u>PJ Harvey – To Bring You My Love</u> Saw the video for *Down By The Water* and cartwheeled out of the house in Yellowknife to custom-order the CD. Every song rocks. I'm always scared when I see Polly Jean Harvey in action: she's so skinny I keep thinking she'll collapse any second and yet she's so full of voodoo when she sings. Where does she find the strength to rock and rage like that? And yet I bet she has the softest kiss.

24. <u>Placebo – Without You I'm Nothing</u> Best album I've heard in years. Soft, tender, hard and cruel. You can feel the lead singer slipping away to heroin's grip. He's trying, really trying to capture any kind of beauty in this album and succeeds. It's honest and brilliant. I just hope he's around to do another album again. The little lost Goth inside me adores the suffering that every song purrs with.

25. <u>Afghan Whigs – (Tie!) Gentleman and 1965</u> Ladies and gentlemen, we have a tie. When I saw the video for *Gentlemen* I flew to the Groove Shop located downtown Penticton and bought it. This is a kick ass album that you can put on "repeat" and live your days out quite nicely. Every song flows with guilt, sin and hard living. I immediately went on a reconnaissance mission to find everything The Whigs ever did before this and, you know what? It's pretty lame. I wish now I had never done it. I was so jaded from my collection of early work I didn't bother to buy the album after *Gentlemen*. When Michelle brought home their latest (*1965*) I didn't want to listen to it. Thank God she did! *1965* matched *Gentlemen* perfectly. It's like they made both albums at the same time. Awesome albums from a band struggling with itself and where it wants to go. And there's a new element I haven't heard in Greg Dulli's voice before: lust. Any woman who can listen to 66 and not throw their panties at the speakers has got to be deaf or dead. They lost me with their albums, *Up In It* and *Congregation*, but brought me back inside their grace with *1965*. Hallelujah!

GERRY WILLIAM

IRON YELLS

Thursday afternoon. Overcast and humid. Several times during the day I looked out through the bars to the river which wound to the ocean ten miles away. The traffic which went by below the front gates seemed a world away. On most days, this being the coast, the rain was a sheet of drops that beat incessantly against the concrete and steel walls. On most days, too, inmates went about their mind-numbing routines, caged by guards ground into sarcastic mean-spirited sets of keys and obscenities.

I'd just delivered a set of library books to the East Wing, where books like Falconer disappeared from cell to cell, turning up six months later in the West Wing or the Center Dome, tossed onto the concrete floors where they knew it would be picked up by some bureaucrat. I'd been the victim again of the guards' contempt, and it was this contempt which kept me from harm—the inmates knowing what the guards were doing. Delivering the books to a tier, I was half-way down the tier when the doors to the tier were unlocked and inmates spilled into the narrow walkway. I hand-delivered the books to an inmate, who turned to throw the books onto the narrow steel-framed cot as I made my patient way to where the guards stood, their eyes glinting as I walked around them.

Leaving the Main Building I ignored the low obscenities of the guards, who regarded people like me in Social Development as 'bleeding hearts.' "Fucking Chief" was the kindest of the words thrown at me on my routes through the prison maze.

I skirted the Main Building, looking forward to pay day tomorrow. The walls loomed fifty feet above me, lined with windows which, only fourteen months before, had witnessed the taking of hostages in the 'bleeding hearts' building by, among others, an Indian contract killer named Sam, considered one of the most dangerous inmates in Canadian history. Following the killing of Anna L., a 'bleeding heart' counselor, by those who stormed into the building, Sam was in the hole—solitary confinement.

Someone had recently been accused in an interview of exaggerating the conditions within the Prison, as it was called, to which the interviewee had shrugged and said it was impossible and useless to exaggerate the situation—for the situation was beyond anything which then existed in Canada. Its only parallel was Alcatraz in the United States.

I knew every part of the Main Building, except for solitary confinement. The system had argued successfully that, given my youth (I was twenty-five then, the average age of any guard) and my ancestry (I was, of course, Aboriginal), I should not be allowed into Solitary, where I suppose I would fall under the influence of Sam, even then being stripped of his humanity (what there was left of it) under the relentless kindness of the guards.

At the midway point of the Main Building exquisitely manicured lawns and flower beds flanked a series of stone steps. Rails split the stone path into two, leaving just room enough on either side for one person at a time to descend or ascend. At the bottom of the steps squatted the Main Gate, large enough to allow military and police vehicles into the prison once they'd been searched.

Did I say that the walls here, as within the Main Building, were reinforced cement walls with steel rebars? The walls were two feet thick. Persistent rumors said that bodies were hidden within those mute walls. Stories within stories.

As I walked down the steps, the first thing I noticed was the lack of inmates tending the flowers and shrubs. A gust of wind from the unseen river fouled the air with sludge from the innumerable pulp mills.

One thing I now remember, one horror, is that for the first time in weeks or months, I noticed the guards on the towers, guards who kept rifles pointed at anyone who walked the inner walls, whether they were workers or inmates.

Half-way down the steps, I felt nervous, my attention on the towers. Behind me came the sound of a car crash. A loud bang of metal against concrete and then, several seconds later, the scream. The gates in front of me swung shut and my supervisor in the long flat building which we worked in shouted for me to get in. I knew better than to run, and walked swiftly towards him. I was ten feet from him when the East Wing, the part of the building I'd just left, erupted into a prolonged frantic series of crashes and the sounds of obscenities, screams and out-of-control laughter.

In the movies, sirens wailing during a prison riot always seem exciting, an adventure. In real life, that initial scream was triggered by prisoners who began to tear apart the walls between their cells with anything they could lay their hands on. The guards began locking down as many cells and tiers as they could, but the inmates rapidly gained control of the East Wing. It took the time between the first scream and the time I reached the door to the building where I worked for the sirens to go off.

The sirens are meant to paralyze. Their high-pitched wails scramble the mind, or are intended to do so. You can hear the sirens ten miles away, and our building was a hundred feet from the nearest siren.

Everybody who works in a maximum security prison has a position to go to in case of emergency. I was in mine, safely within the walls of the Social Development Building, looking out along with the other workers as a stream of guards ran down the same steps I had just walked. There was no use talking to one another; we couldn't hear ourselves if we screamed.

The next few hours were a blur, leading to the time the Army and RCMP encircled the prison walls, leading to the time when we in the building were led out under escort to the Main Gates, where we were put into a secured room next to where inmates received their visitors during good times; leading to the declaration by the Warden that we were on Emergency Duty, which meant we were not allowed to leave the Pen until further orders.

I believe I was scared during those first few hours, but I can't say how scared, because I spent the next two weeks within the walls, every hour spent in fear which became numb, a persistent itch which wouldn't go away. The work was hard, but the fear is what dragged me down, the fear and the hate which colored each and every moment during those initial minutes which led into days and weeks.

Memories sometimes jar things loose in your life, creating a hybrid of mixed emotions and energies which transform the person within times measured often between heartbeats.

Other memories resonate, surfacing at unexpected moments throughout your life, unbidden and all the stronger for it. Memories of tea from childhood generated a 3000-page series of novels in France. There is no single outcome from such memories, just a framework which often reminds you of the power of the imagination, the emotions lying beyond rationality, an ocean waiting to be plundered because it has no limits. My prison moment is one of those memories which continue to affect me, and remind me of how much there is in life which is good and not good, but always there.

I think there is no final message in those moments, just the power of time and people.

BIOGRAPHIES

Jeannette Armstrong

Jeannette Armstrong is from the Penticton Indian Reserve of the Okanagan Nation. She is a graduate of the University of Victoria and founder/ Director of the En'owkin International School of Writing. She is a renowned visual artist, activist, educator and author. Jeannette is a highly sought after speaker and consultant, travelling around the world speaking on Native issues, related to Indigenous rights. She was recently distinguished with an Honourary Doctorate of Letters from St. Thomas University, Fredericton.

Dorothy Christian

Dorothy was born into the Okanagan-Shuswap Nations and is a member of the Spallumcheen Band. She is the eldest of ten children. Dorothy is committed to the revitalization and healing of Indigenous communities through culturally appropriate traditions and contemporary mediums. She has a diverse background in corporate and public administration, fundraising & sales. While in Ontario Dorothy served the Ontario Film Review Board and the Native Canadian Centre Board. Currently, Dorothy is a segment producer for SKYLIGHT, VISION TV's daily human affairs program.

Sylvia Coleman

Sylvia is a member of the Mississaugas of Scugog Island First Nation in Ontario. Her diverse background includes earning a BSC in Environmental Science in Australia. Sylvia then returned to McGill University and earned a BA in Anthropology and thereafter decided to synthesize her creative/cultural and analytical physical sciences interests towards a masters of Architecture at the University of British Columbia.

Beth Cuthand

Beth is a Cree born in La Ronge, Saskatchewan. She attended the University of Regina where she received her Bachelor of Arts Degree on Sociology, she then earned a Master of Fine Arts Degree in Creative Writing from the University of

Arizona. Her many columns and stories of writing have appeared in UBCIC News, Indian World , Saskatchewan Indian, and From the Pipe and Tomorrow File. She wrote and produced twenty-five scripts for CBC Radio's Our Native Land, as well as scripts for various television programs. Cuthand has published her own books, Horse Dance to Emerald Mountain (1987) and Voices in the Waterfall (Theytus Books, 1989) with a 2nd expanded edition (1992)

Chris T. George

My name is Chris George. I am a member of the Miq'maq Nation at Eel River Bar in New Brunswick. I am twenty-four years old and a student at the University of New Brunswick.

i am a miqmaq person... as such my culture is a spoken culture... i changed my style of writing to fit my culture... although my words are written, i write them as i would speak them... and with the same sentimentality in which i view the world... i do not capitalize my words because i see all parts of creation as equal... i do not use sentence structure because i feel that the use of periods does not allow for change, and we are always changing... my use of three dots is symbolic of continuous thought, meaning that i write until i am finished... and leaving those dots is leaving a little room for improvement as i age and grow wiser... thank you for understanding.

nicole (migizikwe) betu

Migizi kwe n-dja-na-koss. I am a Saulteau/Cree/Franco woman. I was born and reared in the foothills of the Rocky Mountains, in Northeastern B.C. Treaty 8 area, Upper Peace River Country. I completed my undergraduate work at Trent University, with a major in Native Studies. I am involved in the Master of Arts Degree Program in Indigenous Governance MAIG, at the University of Victoria. My spiritual and textual passion lies within fine arts and textual expression.

Geary Hobson

Geary Hobson (Cherokee-Quapaw/Chicksaw) is a professor of English, who now lives in Norman Oklahoma. He is the author of <u>Deer Hunting and Other Poems</u> (1990) and the editor of <u>The Remembered Earth: An Anthology of Contemporary Native American Literature</u>(1979). He has served since 1991 as the project historian of Returning the Gift, otherwise known as the Native Writers Circle of the Americas (NWCA).

Roberta Kennedy

Roberta Kennedy is Haida and Squamish. She was born and raised on *Haida Gwaii*. She tells Haida stories and sings Haida songs to audiences of all ages. Her favourite audience is her family (her husband and three Raven children). She currently lives in Edmonton.

Tracey Lindberg

Tracey Lindberg is a Cree woman from Northern Alberta. She is auntie to Kelsey, Michael and Brandon and a daughter to Warren Lindberg and Gloria Belcourt. She works as a Professor of Criminal Justice and Native Studies at Athabasca University and has a law degree from the University of Saskatchewan and a Masters of Law from Harvard University.

Laura Marsden

Laura A. Marsden is an Ojibway/Anishnaabe artist and storyteller from Scugog Island and Rama Reserve in Ontario, Canada. Her art and story represent traditional and contemporary themes of innate legendary quality. Ms. Marsden's lifetime "dreamworks" are representative of a historic and cultural perspective which is influenced by environment, politics and ceremony. "From the cultural fires of the Great Elders, we as messengers preserve the culture and thereby improve the 'Indian Condition' through sanction, accuracy and progression.

Rasunah Marsden

Artistic Statement:

The Anishnaabe were known as 'The Good People.' Literature embodies the essentials of life through storytelling. Words or phrases which struck me in literature led me to the fascinating idea of 'living letters,' or words which had a life of their own; even the spaces or silences between words and in languages speak from within or outside the power of all human relations, community & natural nobility of existence.

Bio:

Of Anishnaabe and French heritage, Rasunah Marsden was born in Brandon, Manitoba. Rasunah received a Bachelor of Arts in English Literature from Simon Fraser University in 1974. She also completed teacher certification & course work for a Masters in Fine Arts in Creative Writing at the University of British Columbia.

After travelling to Australia in 1982 'to discover other states of mind,' Rasunah spent seven years in Jakarta, Indonesia, where she taught English language courses, worked in Telemedia, a tech-transfer company and for Matari Advertising. In 1990, she moved back to Australia, where she received a Post Graduate Diploma of Design from the University of Technology in Sydney, Australia in 1993. Returning to Canada in 1995, she currently teaches creative writing at the En'owkin International School for Writing in Penticton, BC.

Sharron Proulx-Turner

Sharron Proulx-Turner is a member of the Métis Nation of Alberta. Her ancestry includes Mohawk, Huron, Algonquin, French and Irish. Sharron has published one book under the pseudonym Becky Lane entitled <u>Where the Rivers Join: A Personal Account of Healing From Ritual Abuse</u>, with an introduction by Lee Maracle. Sharron has recently written two more books under her own name which are both patiently seeking publication. Her current plan is also to publish a book of interviews with Métis Elders of Alberta. She has two young (used to be children), Graham and Barb. She now lives in Calgary where she writes and teaches.

Janet Rogers

Janet Rogers is a self-taught visual artist and a member of the Mohawk Nation from the Six Nations territory in Southern Ontario. Janet has published chapbooks of poetry she has created under the name of Savage Publishing. Other publications include a sixty page chapbook published by Fine Words. Janet has incorporated spoken word into her readings which are expressed in spoken word performances. Her artwork graces the pages of her latest book entitled <u>Mixed Meditations of an Urban Indian</u>. Janet is currently writing a play, which will feature E. Pauline Johnson and Emily Carr. Her short stories have been included in Native anthologies in British Columbia and Ontario.

Armand Garnet Ruffo

Armand Garnet Ruffo (Ojibway) is the author of a collection of poetry, <u>Opening in the Sky</u> (Theytus Books, 1994) and a poetic biography,<u> Grey Owl: the Mystery of Archie Belaney</u> (Coteau, 1997).

A new collection of poetry, <u>At Geronimo's Grave</u>, will appear in the spring of 2001 from Coteau Books.

His plays include "Portrait of the Artist as An Indian" and "A Windigo Tale," as well as an adaptation of his book on Grey Owl. Ruffo's poetry, stories and essays have appeared in numerous literary journals and anthologies including, <u>Voices of the First Nations</u> (McGraw-Hill Ryerson, 1996), <u>Literary Pluralities</u> (broadview, 1998), <u>An Anthology of Canadian Native Literature in English</u> (Oxford, 1998) <u>Native North America</u> (ECW, 1999), and <u>An Introduction to Literature</u> (Nelson, 2000).

He is currently the Director of the Centre for Aboriginal Education, Research and Culture, and Assistant Professor in the Department of English Language and Literature at Carleton University.

Russell Teed

Russell Teed is a Métis from Yellowknife. He is a former graduate of the En'owkin International School of writing. Russell is currently enrolled in the University of Victoria in the Masters of Public Administration program. His submission "Father" is his personal view of a part of his life recreated creatively. It is a story about his father's death, growing pains and the birth of his children—and ultimately his inner peace, which incorporates the four seasons.

Richard Van Camp

Richard Van Camp is a member of the Dogrib Nation. He is the author of a novel, The Lesser Blessed, and two children's books: A Man Called Raven and What's The Most Beautiful Thing You Know About Horses? illustrated by George Littlechild. His radio play "Mermaids" was narrated by Ben Cardinal and broadcast several times for CBC Radio's 1998 "Festival of Fiction."

Gerry William

Gerry is member of the Spallumcheem Indian Band in South central British Columbia. His novel, The Black Ship, published by Theytus Books, is the first of a series of novels under the general title "Enid Blue Starbreaks." Gerry is also a sessional instructor in English, History, and Creative Writing at NVIT. He has been enrolled in Ph.d program with the Union Institute in Cincinati, Ohio for the past year. As part of his thesis he is writing a novel based on the first contact between the North Okanagan People & European Settlers.

MEMBER OF THE SCABRINI GROUP

Quebec, Canada
2000